Radically Content

BEING SATISFIED IN AN ENDLESSLY DISSATISFIED WORLD

Jamie Varon

ROCK POINT

Inspiring | Educating | Creating | Entertaining

Brimming with creative inspiration, how-to projects, and useful information to enrich your everyday life, quarto.com is a favorite destination for those pursuing their interests and passions.

First published in 2022 by Rock Point, an imprint of The Quarto Group,
142 West 36th Street, 4th Floor, New York, NY 10018, USA
T (212) 779-4972 F (212) 779-6058 www.Quarto.com

Rock Point titles are also available at discount for retail, wholesale, promotional, and bulk purchase. For details, contact the Special Sales Manager by email at specialsales@quarto.com or by mail at The Quarto Group, Attn: Special Sales Manager, 100 Cummings Center Suite 265D, Beverly, MA 01915 USA.

Library of Congress Control Number: 2021947846

10 9 8 7 6 5 4 3 2 1

ISBN: 978-1-63106-847-8

Publisher: Rage Kindelsperger
Creative Director: Laura Drew
Senior Managing Editor: Cara Donaldson
Editor: Keyla Pizarro-Hernández
Cover Design: Joanne O'Neill
Interior Design: Rebecca Pagel

Image Credits:
Cover: thawats/iStock; shunli zhao/Getty Images; Gaby Wojciech/Getty Images; Dole08/iStock; Tarkhanov/iStock; Topaz777/iStock; Bogdan Lytvynenko/iStock.
Interior pages: shunli zhao/Getty Images page 1. kikk/Shutterstock pages 2-3, 6, 20-21, 22, 33, 45, 60, 72, 84, 97, 107, 121, 134-135, 136, 143, 153, 160, 169, 178, 183, 194. thawats/iStock pages 1, 3, 20, 22, 45, 84, 134, 153, 160, 178, 183, 194. Gaby Wojciech/Getty Images pages 33, 60, 107, 134, 135, 136, 178, 194. Dole08/iStock pages 33, 72, 97, 134, 153, 178, 183, 194. Tarkhanov/iStock pages 20, 22, 33, 143, 178, 194. Topaz777/iStock pages 45, 72, 134, 153, 183, 194. Bogdan Lytvynenko/iStock pages 6, 20, 33, 121, 135, 169, 194.

Printed in China

This book is dedicated to
the nonconformists,
rebels, and sensitive souls.

MAY WE CONTINUE TO BE

BOLD, BRAVE, AND OPEN.

CONTENTS

PART 2
TO LEARN . . .

An Endlessly Dissatisfied World

I CANNOT MAKE SENSE of the deep inequity in our world. How happiness is reserved only for the elite few who are born in the right country, with the right skin tone, with the right kind of opportunities, in the right kind of body. How can the pinnacle of the human experience, the one that we all compare and contrast with, be so inaccessible to most of the world's population? How come we are told that massive achievement and unbelievable wealth are what make us happy, and yet the people who have that kind of power are often the most cruel, heartless, and punishing people? It's like we are all under a spell that we have never thought to interrogate. (Myself included, for many, *many* years.)

So many people are often unhappy, feeling as though their life hasn't amounted to their potential, mostly because they are comparing to an ideal. Many people feel as though they are living some parallel life—a sadder one, a harder one, a less-than one—because other people have so much more than they have.

Often, we take societal conditioning as ultimate truth. And yet, it's not. We've been socialized to both care about and uphold a value system that has been handed to us, and reinforced, since birth. A value system that places emphasis on a hierarchy that purports that as long as someone is "below" us, we are doing okay in life. We take this societal value system on, and it becomes synthesized as our own truth. We ingest and absorb it. And that value system becomes how we measure the significance of our own life, how much happiness we allow ourselves to have, how much we feel we are doing "well." This hierarchy is killing our humanity.

Body standards have changed throughout the years, and yet there's always been a standard that everyone aims to achieve. Wealth has always been distributed unevenly, and the more uneven it gets, the more normalized that inequity becomes. People feel like failures for not thriving in a broken world, in broken systems, in corruption, in a world where many countries elevate profit above humanity. People feel like they are failing in a system that expects them to be robots—productive, perfect, unfeeling, and without emotional needs.

Often, what we think we need and want isn't a true, genuine desire. It's a reach for social capital. Because in our current world, social capital means more than anything else. Have the right body, the right look, the right skin color, the right sexual orientation, the right belief system, the right everything—and you will be fine. Everyone else will have to either grapple with a sense of feeling inadequate or be forced to spend years unlearning their own self-hatred. A self-hatred that was given to them by a narrow-minded society that wants to make happiness and worth a matter of deserving—who deserves it more? We have created a system that makes people fight for, claw for, and suffer for their worth. We have created hierarchies of humanity so that only the ones at the top are supposedly living "well."

It's a bad system.

It's a bad system because *nobody* seems to be very happy. Even the people at the top. They are usually ruthless, power-hungry, greedy, self-serving. And when you are those things, you have lost your connection to humanity. When you are that type of person, you cannot connect to others. So, you may have your riches at the top of the mountain, but what else do you have? What do you have of worth that cannot be bought?

And what about all the many billions of people who are not accumulating the world's resources in a fight for power? We lose, too. We *are* losing. If there's one thing that 2020 showed me in Technicolor lights, it's that this world, and especially Western culture, does not care about its people. It doesn't care about the well-being of anyone, not really. If people get in the way of profits, that can't happen. If the planet gets in the way of profits, burn it down. We do not hold each other. We do not care for each other. It's everyone for themselves. There is no sense of community or care. There might be pockets of it, but it's not the value system of most of the Western world.

And we are all suffering for it.

In many ways, this is a self-growth book. Self-help. Self-transformation. Whatever you want to call it.

This book is meant to help *you* find healing, but it's also about healing the world.

BEING RADICALLY CONTENT starts with emotionally opting out of the world. Unlearning the value system of a harsh and power-hungry society—and creating a new *internal* value system where you are affirmed, seen, worthy, loved. Once you start to opt out of a society that does not want you to be happy or valued as you are, it's like waking up from a bad dream. And it's also freeing. You don't have to see yourself as "falling behind" because that is now a construct created to keep you doubting yourself. You don't have to be a commodity. You don't have to do more and be more in order to earn external appreciation, which you hope will lead to internal love. You don't have to do your life *their* way in any way at all. You don't have to follow the rules of society. (The laws, yes, even when some of the laws are grossly unjust.) You can opt out. *Radically.*

The opt out starts within. It's a mind-set change. Then it becomes behavioral change. How that looks for me will look drastically different from how it looks for you. Everyone's opt out will lead them to the life that is radically meant for them.

Opting out looks like having your own value system. Ending the compulsion to compare. Loving yourself. Caring about what you think about *yourself,* not what other people think about you. The opt out is the cornerstone of a radically content life. It means denying what the world wants from you in favor of what you want from you. The opt out is about you building the life that makes you feel most fulfilled, healing from a harsh, demanding world—and no longer living within the confines of *their* "rules."

The opt out is radical freedom.

Where you don't have to prove another damn thing to anyone. You don't have to strive for your worth. You don't have to wait for the world to affirm you. You don't have to wait for your life to begin. You don't need permission from anyone at all.

Radically content is a way of life. But it's not *my* way of life. It's living *your* way of life. It's defining success for *you.* It's being happy in the simplicity of your life. It's being done with striving and proving and earning your own worth and measuring your value by the standards of a broken and ruthless world.

It's about living not based on societal conditioning or what culture tells you to value and want. But what you, inside—in your truest, deepest self—desire.

It's you, stripped away from who the world has told you to be.

It's you, at your freest, most expressed self.

Radically content is an unlearning. An unbecoming. A shedding. A healing. A whole-making.

And it's also a movement.

Because it's a way for us all to be happy, no matter where we are or who we are. It's an invitation. It's a way out of the brutal demands of the world.

It's a way for happiness, satisfaction, and contentment to include *more* of us. It's an invitation into the most inclusive spot. Where we all belong. Where we're all worthy. Where nobody has to try to do or be anything more than who they are. Where you don't have to be the best, or build an empire, or win awards, or do anything you don't truly desire to do just to prove how good you are at keeping up.

My hope is that enough of us opting out will start a change. We keep trying to be good in a system that doesn't care about us. We keep trying to win within a system where winning means exploiting. We keep trying to get something *out there* that is waiting to be noticed within. This game is not meant to be *won*.

If enough of us opt out, a tide will shift.

This book is a radical invitation to be exactly who you are and opt out of, shed, let go, and heal from anything that's telling you that who you are isn't good enough.

From that foundation, you can build. Construct a life that fits you perfectly. It's a letting go so it can come together again.

It's a you thing.

And it's also an us thing.

We're all in this together.

Nobody deserves a beautiful life that they love more than you.

Or me.

Or us.

To write a book about being happy and content—it feels deeply uncool. I used to love my pessimism, my skepticism, my rallying cries that being happy is just delusion. I thought my negativity gave me edge. I thought my anxiety propelled me to better art, better achievements. I spent my twenties wanting to be cool, like the writers in Brooklyn cafes who wear black turtlenecks and drink coffee black and write from laptops in front of exposed brick walls.

I never wanted to be earnest. Sentimental. Or happy.

Happy felt like giving up. Contentment felt like settling. I was supposed to be *special*. Sad, but accomplished. Anxious, but impressive. I didn't want to *inspire* anyone. I wanted to be *better* than everyone. I didn't want to be relatable. Or joyful. Or okay. Or healthy.

And yet, I landed in my thirties feeling supremely hopeless, apathetic, unhappy, restless, and frustrated. There was no joy in my life. I had no optimism. I hated people who were happy. Hated them. I lived in my complaints. I argued for all my limitations. I felt entitled to the success I was *meant* for, that I needed, that I thought would finally make me worthy.

I wanted it all. To be unhappy, yet happy. To be edgy, yet light. To be cool, yet earnest.

I grew up in the 1990s. As a teenager, you weren't supposed to be nice or kind. To not care was to be cool. I wanted deeply not to care, to be unaffected, to be one of those writers who writes about the Real Shit. Depressing shit. Anxious shit. Depressing shit again.

But, then I realized: *I'm* depressed. I'm anxious. I'm sad. I'm pessimistic. I'm hurting me. My not-caring means I'm not caring about *myself*. My irony isn't funny. My complaints don't give me an edge. I'm just harming myself.

Now I am earnest, sincere, compassionate, light, and caring. I care so deeply. I want things. I am positive. I believe in affirmations. I am the bright, sunny person I used to hate.

And I don't care.

Because in the end, I am happy.

And I want to feel good. I want to be happy. I want to continue to heal. I want to be a person who understands the intricacies of joy. I want to be content. And satisfied. I am deeply earnest now.

And I suspect you are, too, even if you don't know it.

Welcome.

***

ON THE CUSP OF EVERY BIG TRANSFORMATION, there's a turning point. It's not fluttery and fun. It's often painful. Most of us don't change until we've hit the point when it's untenable not to.

I'm not a naturally happy person. Beneath my hard-earned sunny disposition lives a person prone to negativity, anxiety, complaints, dissatisfaction, and general unease about the world and her place within it.

I am existentially in crisis most of the time.

But I am also stubbornly in love with life.

It's a paradox I've been trying to reconcile for thirty-six years now. A buzzing between there must be *more* than this and I must make the *most* of this.

At the end of 2016, I started taking an antianxiety medication. I knew I didn't want to be on it forever. So, I made a sobering vow that even to this day I'm surprised I took so seriously. It's not like I was a habitual person. I'd been breaking my own promises for a couple of decades by that point. But, something about the confluence of the medication and my overwhelming anxiety meant that I had to take myself seriously.

So, I made myself a vow.

I would take my antianxiety medication, but I'd also do anything and everything within my power to make myself happy. I'd heal from my past. I'd get out of debt. I'd journal. I'd exercise. I'd quit every stressful ambition. I'd find a way to like myself and my life just as it is. I'd accept where I am, even though where I am is nothing like where I wanted to be in my thirties. I quieted my ambition for a while. The same ambition that had been pushing me for so long. The ambition that was eating me up, using a constant feeling of dissatisfaction as fuel. I quit everything that wasn't making me happy.

All I wanted was to be happy.

To feel good.

I realized that I'd never had that singular goal before.

I'd been trying to *achieve* my way into happiness, the way that society tells us to do.

And I was exhausted by it.

I had nothing left to give. I was thirty-one years old, and I had been grinding and hustling for so long that I didn't know what I even wanted any longer. It all just felt like pressure. A mounting, unsustainable, panicked pressure.

All of 2017, I took my antianxiety medication every morning, the first habit I ever truly consistently kept, and I started to experiment. I whittled my life down to only the necessities. I made money to survive, to pay the bills, and to pay off debt, forgoing all my passion projects. I stopped having ten side hustles. I simplified. It felt like giving up. It felt like failing. But there was a surprising clarity in my singular focus. Eventually, I'd be happy. I couldn't understand how, because I always thought you had to keep earning and achieving in order to get there.

But this felt like a step in the right direction. A sort of divine intervention. I trusted the wisdom within my body that told me to slow down. It wasn't so much a choice, but a necessity. The life I was living before was harming me—and I was deeply bone-tired of harming myself.

That's where this book begins. At the beginning of 2017, in what I thought was going to be a quick stopover into a larger journey, but in actuality became the foundation for my life.

At the time, I didn't realize that what I was building was a contented, satisfied life. That I was deprogramming myself from the hustle and decades of societal conditioning. That I was learning how to accept exactly where I am and build a life that I don't need to regularly disassociate, escape, and distract from.

I didn't know where I was headed, but in the dark tunnel of that trust that things could get better, I found an entire way of living outside the norms of society.

A contented, satisfied life.

A *radically* content life.

A life that includes all my most honest dreams and desires, but doesn't delay the enjoyment of the present moment. A life that doesn't wait to earn my joy, relaxation, or health. A life that isn't out of balance skewed in favor of trying to accomplish my way into self-worth.

In that sense, contentment is not about living without dreams or hopes. Contentment, to me, is not complacency. It's not settling.

It's about living fully expressed, not delaying my joy for the promise of some future check mark that society has told me to want. When you are content with where you are, it doesn't make you *less* motivated. It makes you motivated by the *right* things. It makes you motivated by love, passion, enjoyment, genuine desire—and you aren't striving for worthiness.

Being satisfied in my life as it is right here, right now gives me open, fertile space to transform and grow. Achievement, dreams, accomplishment—all of that becomes the cherry on top of an already wonderful life. It's absolutely possible to be both ambitious and content. To me, this is a new and radical way to live outside of our productivity and achievement-obsessed culture. Our happiest life isn't some destination we have to earn our way into. It's an unfolding—and we are constantly evolving.

Contentment isn't giving up. It's a foundation.

It's the foundation I believe most of us search for, but don't know it.

This book is the journey—how you can go from being trapped in the hustle culture mentality to being genuinely happy where you are. It includes all the lessons I picked up along the way. Each chapter in part 1 focuses on a concept to unlearn and opt out of in order to transition into a radically content life. Following that is part 2—practical concepts to learn that can lead you further into your journey. All of it—every single part—is meant to lead *you* deeper into *yourself*.

This book is not me telling you *exactly* what to do.

It's me leading you to understanding what you already know.

This book is for people who, like me, are ambitious, have high hopes and big dreams for their life, but who also want to *enjoy* their life. The ones who know there *has* to be a better way. We exist in the balance. The nuance. We can't be put in a box.

So, here's what I'll say before you get into this book: I have no desire to put you in a box. But let this book be a guide. It's the guide I wished I had at many points in my life. A way to work and live and exist that honors our truest selves, brings us satisfaction and joy in our daily lives, and still leaves wide open space for expansion and growth and the realization of all our dreams.

Here's to us.

May we never delay our joy ever again.

A NOTE ON PRIVILEGE

EVEN THOUGH I WROTE THIS BOOK with the intention to help you find healing, I'm aware of the harm that can be caused by oversimplifying self-help concepts. Coming from a white middle-class family in Northern California, I grew up with humble beginnings in the context of my hometown, but in the broader global context, I was afforded privileges that I know many in the world don't have access to. While I have done my absolute best to be as sensitive as possible to all the variance and levels of privilege that exist in this world, I know that I cannot fully encapsulate the tapestry of humanity and the full spectrum of your experience. I strive, in all my work, to be as inclusive as possible. I hope that endeavor is reflected here and that this book will serve as a source of healing and comfort to you.

PART 1

To Unlearn...

EVERY BIG TRANSFORMATION starts with awareness. Awareness is one of the most powerful tools in our lives. Without being conscious of our environment and the subtle messages we're consuming, we may live on autopilot, subconsciously trying to keep up with values we don't personally have. If only we'd slow down enough to know ourselves intimately.

In this section, I've provided concepts that are vital to unlearn in a dissatisfied world. Just the unlearning of these concepts can make a drastic impact on the quality of your life. How you interpret your life is how you experience your life. When you can change the filter in which you see yourself and your life, it's freedom. And often, the very thing you were trying to escape was not just a situation, but a belief that has kept you circling the same challenge.

In this unlearning, you may be surprised by where your life takes you. Your dreams may shift. Your ambitions may change. You may find yourself reclaiming lost desires. You may find yourself constructing a whole new narrative for yourself. My hope is that you embrace it. Free yourself from who the world has told you to be—and powerfully take the life that is meant for you. Whatever path the unlearning leads you down, know it's *yours*. It won't look like mine, and that's the point. I want you to discover the beauty of your own life—and fall in love with it.

Unlearning who the world has told you to be is healing. It's you reclaiming your own narrative. It's you reclaiming your own life. It's you taking back your mind from conformist thinking. Let's get into it.

CHAPTER 1

Being Dissatisfied Is Normal

MOST OF US HAVE CONVINCED OURSELVES that dissatisfaction is a correct response to our current life. Dissatisfaction becomes our motivation to creating our happiness. Sometimes our perpetual dissatisfaction can feel like the natural conclusion for a life that we feel isn't living up to its potential. In many ways, contentment can feel like giving up. Settling. Who wants to be *satisfied* if you can be striving? Crush it! Never give up! Make it! Never stop! No bad days! Good vibes only! You'll sleep when you're dead!

For years, I was assured that my dissatisfaction was actually at the crux of my drive. If I *like* myself, won't I just give up on all my endeavors? Pursuing, achieving, proving, striving—all of that felt so much more urgent than being happy, or content.

I didn't have the "right" body. I wasn't yet in the career I had dreamed of. I wasn't the best. I didn't have romantic prospects coming at me constantly. I hadn't built any kind of empire.

My dissatisfaction was the *least* I could offer for having not fulfilled the dreams of my younger self. For not "measuring up."

Dissatisfaction in myself and my life wasn't a conclusion I came to on my own like I believed. It was a *learned* conclusion. A socialized feeling. It was conditioning.

There's a lot of money to be made off of people feeling bad about themselves. When there is an ideal and a standard that is fed to us all from a very young age, we will instinctively want to become it—and if a company seems to have the solution, we'll buy it.

Cultivating a dissatisfied world is a very profitable endeavor. What money can be made off satisfied, content people? Not much.

But our self-doubt? Our perpetual malaise? The conditioning to keep up with others? Now, that's a goldmine.

If the ideal is an ever-moving target, even better. More money. More problems to create that they can sell the solutions for. This isn't a conspiracy theory. It's the basis for modern advertising. I was a marketing student, and they teach this in consumer behavior. They call the problems your "pain points" and persuade you into thinking that their specific product can counteract it. In creating a "need" for their product, they've also created an issue for people to internalize. And in a capitalist society, that means a lot of pain points that were manufactured to create a need for products we probably don't need at all.

Because products are created to provide solutions, sometimes the reason for the solution has to be created, too. Without any knowledge that this dissatisfaction is being pumped into the very air we breathe, it's hard to know what is yours to carry—and what is something that has been ingrained over the years.

It didn't occur to me that I could think any differently. I knew that I felt bad. I knew that my depression was overwhelming, a sinking blackness that would have me disassociate from reality for weeks at a time. I knew that I did not like myself.

But I didn't know another woman in existence who didn't also feel the same way as me.

So, I thought it was normal.

Everywhere I went, headlines from magazines would jump out at me. Solutions for your love life, body, and life "problems"— some I didn't have, but managed to adopt just from the exposure to it in the grocery store. Messaging I picked up, just from existing in the world. Even if I didn't consciously consume something, it was everywhere. It was in every conversation with a friend, every complaint about our bodies and our lives, a chorus of similar messaging that felt like facts.

That you wouldn't be loved in a larger body.

That you wouldn't have the best life if you didn't become smaller.

That you aren't allowed to be happy until you achieved a certain set of things.

That as long as other people approved of you, it didn't matter how you felt about yourself.

That you are a constant self-improvement project—and anything else is lazy.

That hating ourselves is just what women do.

That we're hard on ourselves.

That we doubt ourselves.

That every choice we make isn't the "right" one.

It couldn't possibly be a *culture* that created this environment. No. It was just every single person coming to the same conclusion over the years—that they were never going to be good enough, no matter how hard they worked, how hard they tried, and how hard they hustled.

Right.

As if we all decided to hate ourselves at the exact same time.

As if there isn't an entire culture built on making us feel inferior.

As if we didn't feel the need to compete with each other for the tiniest crumbs.

Eventually, the doubt and dissatisfaction that I learned to adopt as my own stopped being cultural messaging and instead became an internal battle. I had so much evidence that I wasn't good enough. I had taken the external dissatisfaction and made it into my own belief system. I absorbed the societal expectations as if it were my own ideology. As if I woke up one day and decided that my own life wasn't ever going to be good enough.

So then, the solutions started to become appealing to me. I would lose weight and then I'd be okay. I would achieve X and then I'd earn my value. I would do all the things I was supposed to do and one day it'll all click in for me.

One day, I'll be okay.

I don't even know if it was as conscious as that. It was more like: I feel bad about myself, so I need to do anything and everything I can think to do to get *away* from that feeling. I spent so many years trying to escape from myself. Trying to turn away from myself. Trying to be anyone *but* me.

I had no reason to think I shouldn't feel constantly dissatisfied. We, especially women, are expected to dislike our bodies, to never be fully satisfied in the choices we make, to always be "missing" something. Our bodies are never right, and we should always be trying to age youthfully. If we choose careers, we'll regret not having kids. If we stay at home with kids, we'll feel useless without a career. (And all the many variances of shame in between when it comes to having, not having, choosing not to, not being able to—have children.) This messaging is everything. It starts as a cultural conditioning and then we inhale it into a personal belief. As if we would consciously choose to be perpetually and endlessly dissatisfied with our own lives.

I could never understand what the endgame was, but still I pursued it. What was at the end of this elusive rainbow? Some paradise where my perfect body, perfect life, perfect partner, perfect job all culminate into a life that is without pain, or insecurity, or self-hatred? What was I even running *toward*?

I knew what I was running away *from*, but that's all I was doing. Running away.

Running away from that panic in my chest that I wasn't measuring up. Running away from feeling like I was behind. Running away from the swirling sense of dissatisfaction that lingered in my body.

But . . . what was I running *toward*?

What was the reward?

They tell us: the ends justify the means. Miserably slog your way to success. Get that achievement. Never give up. Pain is gain.

But what *for*? What do we *get*? What is the *outcome*?

What is the point, though? The larger point? What are we killing ourselves and wasting our lives to achieve? What do we get? How does it benefit us?

What ends justify the means, if the means are unhappiness, loss of time, loss of enjoyment? What ends are more important than our well-being, our relationships, our mental, physical, and emotional health?

These are the questions I could never answer. Maybe that was the point. Maybe the unanswerable nature of these questions is what made them so tantalizing and elusive. Maybe that's how dissatisfaction breeds into productivity. Maybe that's how you control a whole group of people—by giving them ends they can never meet, like putting a hamster on his little wheel to nowhere.

I knew I hated the way I felt. I knew that the dissatisfaction was overwhelming. But, what else was there? Everyone else seemed to hate themselves, too. Everyone else was doing the same things as me, scrambling for something, hoping to be loved and accepted and seen and chosen. All of us were looking for that out there, somewhere. For an answer. The right solution. Maybe the right person. Something that would take the weight off.

The only solution that seemed to make sense was to work for it. If our dissatisfaction had become the culmination of not being "enough" per societal standards that we internalized as our own, then the logical answer was to somehow become "enough." But of course, "enough" is a murky definition, too. It's impossible to define. It's subjective. It's ethereal and vague. What is "enough" and how do we know when we've reached it?

That's the genius of the dissatisfaction—there's no real way to cultivate the opposite. It's a losing game. We're not ever supposed to find our way out of the labyrinth. It's meant to keep us confused and searching and chasing and striving and hustling and proving. The dissatisfaction does not have a solution. It's an issue with many heads and tangents. It's meant to be unobtainable. It's a problem that is designed to stay a problem. It keeps us addicted to solutions that will never work. And it keeps us thinking that other people get to decide when we are "enough."

We bore these insecurities that are, at the core, simply fears of what other people will think about us. Because we have internalized an idea that all of us need to be the same, look the same, and fall into the same ideal and standard. We end up caring more about what other people think of us and our lives than what we think about ourselves and our lives. It's not because we are weak. It's because we've been *conditioned* to think this way. As if our lives are projections for other people to affirm or deny, living in fear of their disapproval. And living in need of their approval.

"What will they think?" is a four-word question that has killed more dreams and happiness than any other. Who is "they"? And why do we care so much what they think? Who is this faceless group of people that is going to come for us if we don't measure up to their ideal? And why are we not really encouraged to examine this idea we take as absolute incontrovertible truth?

It's exhausting trying to win a game that is designed to be unwinnable.

In an ideal world, we would live in a utopia where everybody is included, heard, and seen, and not one person grows up thinking it's natural and normal to hate themselves. People of all races and sexualities and body types can live freely, without learning how to hate themselves if they don't fit into a narrow view.

But that progress isn't here yet. And until that progress shows up in reality, we need to thrive within our own terms. And my humble hope is that the more of us who stop waiting for the world to change in order to be happy—and bring that happiness to ourselves and others—*that's* what actually does change the world.

If we didn't all opt *into* this system, that robs us of our humanity and joy, then we wouldn't have this value system. The one that says money over people; better for me; best for me. When we all want to be "the best" and dominate over others, what kind of equitable society do you think we're building? We like to look at symptoms of the issue, how it all manifests, and fix those. Fix the inequality. Fix the world. Fix this. But if we don't get to the root of *ourselves*, we can't get to the root of the world's shortcomings either. If we don't understand *where* this inequity comes from, where we lose our own humanity, then we have no way of fixing it.

How do we create a happy, content, and satisfied world if we, ourselves, cannot be these things? Every time you believe a "should" and ignore yourself in favor of listening to societal conditioning, you are conforming to their way of life. I'm not saying it's easy to undo, unlearn, and unfold from that conditioning. But if we don't try, what will ever change?

Here's what I realized over the many years of living within this paradigm, unlearning it, and then successfully living outside of it: we are not required to be dissatisfied. We think it's an inevitability, that nobody really likes themselves or their life very much. We think it's something that has no solution, because so often we look for the solution outside of ourselves. We accumulate and achieve and do all the things we're supposed to do and still the dissatisfaction is present. But that's because there is nothing that the external world can give you when you have to give satisfaction to yourself.

To me, the only way to satisfaction is by a drastic, overwhelming unlearning. The culture that made us sick cannot make us well. So, the only logical solution is to opt out of the culture that is making us unwell.

That means trading in social capital and social privilege for a more authentic and freeing life. It's impossible to gather enough external approval that we can finally be happy. There is no satisfaction in playing the rules, playing their game.

We don't need to be in constant pursuit of our "best" lives. Our most "impressive" lives. A life that is better than someone else's. We do not need to always be hustling. We do not need to spend our life in pursuit of achievements that have no real value to us internally.

For me, the pursuit is in having the freest life. The most expressed. The least held back. I want to be healed. I want to be radically content and radically satisfied. I don't want this world to tell me my worth. I want to derive my worth from inside my own soul. I'm not trying to live the best life that people can aspire to. I am not here to trade in jealousy for profit. I want to be free.

And I want you to be free, too.

The goal is to be the most expressed version of yourself. You should feel free to jump in the pool with your bathing suit on, to wear sleeveless dresses, to love with abandon, to create the art that lights you up, to construct and build an entire life that is so *you*, there's no room for comparison.

You deserve to love your life so much that it doesn't matter who affirms or denies you.

You deserve to find what makes you happy, what brings you joy.

You deserve to feel free, healed, whole.

You deserve to feel your feelings.

You deserve to not let fear stop you.

You deserve to be brave.

You deserve to feel so radically satisfied and content in your own life that you couldn't care less whether anyone approves or disapproves of you.

Unlearn whoever you were taught to be, and become exactly who you are.

Write your own map. And live wildly, completely free.

CHAPTER 2

More Is Always Better

THERE ARE CERTAIN TENETS OF SUCCESS that we adopt without ever interrogating them. "More is better" is the most prevalent one. More success is better. More money is better. More employees are better. More more more must be better. But in so many ways, more is not better. There's a hefty requirement for "more" and it usually means you're going to have to neglect many other areas of your life to get to this pinnacle. And, what do you get when you get there? The knowledge that you beat out everyone else? The ability to buy literally anything you could want, therefore rendering desire as nothing more than accumulation? What value does it hold then?

These are ideals we never interrogate. We simply accept them as an ultimate truth, and either feel bad for ourselves that we aren't there or grind and hustle until we get there. Then whatever there is becomes a moving target.

When I turned thirty, I realized that I wasn't anywhere I expected to be. I couldn't believe that at my age, I was not a full-time writer yet. That I hadn't published a book. I felt like a failure. I felt like everyone who had anointed me with "potential" would now see me as a failure.

So, I accepted a job as a writer at a popular online publication. I took a massive pay cut and worked with people ten years younger than me. But I could tell people I was a "full-time writer." I could post on social media that I got a job as a writer. It was very impressive. People were impressed.

In December 2015, I wrote a post for that website called "This Is How We Date Now," and it went viral. Eventually, this post was read and clicked millions of times. I'd been waiting for my first viral hit since I was hired in April of 2014.

This was supposed to be my dream job. I was being *paid* to write.

But all I felt was anxious.

Anxious about how little I enjoyed it and anxious about what that meant.

And I watched as this essay I'd written was being read by millions of people, something I'd been waiting for, something that had been on my mind for years, a pinnacle of some writerly achievement. It happened. And it was the most disillusioning experience.

Because I didn't suddenly feel capable or without doubt. Actually, my doubt *multiplied*. I couldn't sleep. I checked the charts every single second to make sure my essay hadn't been overtaken by another writer. I was terrified I would never write anything good ever again. I thought back to my twenties and how I put every hope and aspiration into being a writer, and assumed that every problem was borne from the fact that I was not yet a writer. I wondered when I was going to feel happy. When was it going to click in? The happiness I was promised. There I was, achieving what I set out to do. It was very splashy. People from high school who never paid any attention to me were messaging me on Facebook saying they saw this essay floating around.

I'd been waiting for this.

I'd been banking on this.

I'd been sacrificing all my joy for this.

I'd been punishing myself for years for not being *here* yet.

And then I got *here*—and it wasn't at all what I expected.

And it felt like my world was on fire around me.

Because if *this* didn't make me happy, what would?

That job illuminated so much for me. Because that moment where I had impressed everyone flew away in a minute and all that was left was the work of trying to write pithy listicles that would be hate-clicked by millions of people. All that was left was the work of wading through abusive comments, and hoping that I was popular enough to earn my measly salary.

More was not better.

But, everyone thought I had a dream job. So, who cares how it actually was day to day? I was finally a full-time writer! Surely being able to *say* that was more important than actually enjoying the job. (Yeah, it was *not*.)

I quit that job, after a year of stress, frustration, and disappointment. Quitting was difficult because a sad, lonely, unhealed part of me kept asking, "What do you have now without this? You're about to be thirty-one." So, I put all my value and worth into a Facebook page I'd been building with my writing. I watched those numbers like they could make my entire existence feel worthwhile.

And when I received an email from a literary agent who wanted to talk about me doing a book, I took the call as if it were water in an endlessly dry desert. I was desperate for this validation. I can say that now, with the benefit of retrospect, but all of this was happening in a buzzy chaos below the surface. What looked like an incredible opportunity became my most important lesson in what success really is to me.

I signed the agreement. I said yes to the agent. I didn't exactly love their ideas for my potential book, but I didn't care. I had an agent. More importantly, I had something to announce on social media so that nobody thought I was a total failure for quitting a full-time writing job. Did I have a book idea? Did I have the emotional capacity to work on a book? It didn't matter, as long as I could announce to people that I had secured a literary agent—the shininess of that proclamation was *supposed* to be the happiness.

That's what I'd been told: You get these things and you tell people about these things and you get to be happy.

That's what I thought the formula was.

And there I was, anxious about everything, feeling behind, hustling and stressing and striving and proving—waiting for that damn happiness to show up. How much more could I line up and do before I was allowed to be happy?

I spent a year working on a book proposal, discarding ideas and feeling aimless. I'd wake up stressed. I'd go to sleep stressed. I got myself deeper into debt, all on the premise that it was going to be worth it when I got a book deal. *I'll take care of my life when I get a book deal. I'll pay it all off with a windfall advance payment. I need this. I have to have this. Who will I be without a book deal? Nobody. That's who.*

A year passed in that blur—and I became more anxious by the day, the pressure mounting, the expectations like clamped hands around my throat.

I had to make it work. I had to do this. I couldn't be happy if I didn't do this. That's what I thought. That's what I assumed. That's what plagued me every night while I tried to sleep, waking at 3 a.m. to do my anxious worrying.

And then I couldn't do it any longer.

With shaking hands, I made the decision to let go of that agent. Not because there was anything wrong with her, or she was not supportive, but because I was simply not ready. I had spent a year trying to formulate ideas, and I felt that I had lost something essential about myself. I wasn't writing because I felt I had something to say. I was writing to get a book deal. I was writing to tell other people I got a book deal. I was writing because I had something to prove, a validation I needed—and it was causing a significant amount of distress. My marriage was declining. My health was, too. Debt was rising. I felt I was in some sort of trance, like I'd be absolutely nothing or nowhere in life if I let this opportunity go. What would I tell people? That's the first question I asked myself when making a decision that would affect only me.

What would I tell people?

It was like a siren call to myself.

I'd been collecting approval like the accumulation of it would finally prove to me I am good enough. I had become so addicted to the *promise* of success that I didn't think there was anything left to be excited about.

This became the catalyst for 2017, a year that changed the trajectory of my life. It was the year I quit everything—every ambition that was buzzing under my skin to be fulfilled, every goal that kept my mind spinning at night, and every achievement that I thought I needed in order to be happy.

That's when I made the conscious choice to be happy in the right here, right now. When I committed to letting go of whatever was preventing my happiness—and added in only what would amplify it. When I stopped believing that more of everything was always, always better.

By 2018, after intense focus and long hours of design and branding client work, I was out of debt and had a healthy savings account. I hadn't written a single word in a long time, hadn't let any ambitions sneak in. My husband and I decided to move to France for a year, back to where we originally met. Without the noise of my striving and stress, it seemed like the most obvious, exciting decision.

When you have no one left to impress, the real you can start to peek through.

And what I wanted to do more than anything was go to France.

That year really changed everything for me.

When my husband, Houssem, and I decided to go to France, and secured ourselves long-stay visas to do so, I felt a strange and overwhelming anxiety about it. This didn't fit within the story of who you're supposed to be in your thirties. Houssem and I, a married couple, were supposed to settle down, find a home to live in, get a dog, maybe have a child, and live out our lives in that way for the next however many decades. That was what everyone else was doing. That was what was *expected* of us.

I was then thirty-two years old, and many of the people in my social circle either had kids or were on their way. I was about to pack up my entire life in a storage container and go live in a foreign country for no reason other than to just . . . do it. I had a lot of tension about this, so much so that I almost convinced Houssem that we shouldn't go. I felt I was living outside of the bounds, that I was doing something "wrong." Even though I have always been rebellious of the status quo, something about being in my thirties flared up all the conditioning I'd been susceptible to for years. I had this overwhelming sense that I had to do the adulthood settling-down checklist.

And then, simply because of Houssem's fierce desire to travel, we went. I told myself we could come back at any time. My anxiety was heightened. I was terrified of getting back into debt. I wanted to live within the lines, stay in my comfort zone.

We arrived in Paris after a painfully long flight, checked into our Airbnb, had a restless sleep because the Airbnb was nothing like the pictures, and spent the next day untangling ourselves from that apartment and finding something else through a rental agency. I always feel emotionally tender from jet lag, so I was like a live wire. My emotions were right on the surface.

We had to move all our luggage into a tiny hotel room in Montmartre because our apartment wouldn't be ready by Monday. The French do not rush. And they don't work on the weekends if they don't have to, so we were stuck. We collapsed onto the small bed in the small room. I was sweating. I was delirious from exhaustion.

But something had unlocked.

I felt . . . alive.

Truly, ridiculously alive.

Like I was beyond the boxes, beyond the rules, out in some wonderful open expanse where I didn't have to live my life like everyone else. So I didn't have a book deal. So I wasn't a "full-time writer." So I wasn't anywhere I thought I would be by now.

But, who cares? I was in *Paris*.

It felt like I had found a secret door to a secret world that nobody knew about. Yes, I wasn't impressive in all the ways I thought I would be, but I had done something right to be able to work from anywhere, make money, and live in Paris for as long as I pleased. It was an absolute privilege to be able to do this.

That experience of living in Paris for four months and then living in Cannes on the French Riviera for eight changed my entire perception of "success." It didn't matter that I hadn't accumulated all the accolades I thought I should by that age, because I was walking along the Seine without a care in the world. It didn't matter that I wasn't writing, because I was floating in the Mediterranean in warm, crystal-clear water that felt like a baptism.

I realized that a life outside of the perception and conventions of success wasn't going to be one that would drain me—it was going to fill me up completely. The hustle had led me to stress, anxiety, medication, a life that never felt good enough. And the letting go of that expectation had led me here. Whatever had led me to the French Riviera was the life I wanted.

It's the *perception* of success that we get addicted to. Will someone think we've given up if we don't take the promotion? If I'm not doing as well as *this* person, will they think I'm not doing well? If I don't keep accumulating more and more, won't people think I'm not successful? We don't realize it, but often what we're motivated by are external rewards. The external rewards we've been conditioned to care about: how other people view our lives; how impressive we are; how "well" we're doing based on a very narrow definition.

Shockingly, Houssem and I needed *less* money to live in France. It was legitimately cheaper to live on the French Riviera than to live in Los Angeles. And I found myself feeling intense gratitude that I hadn't weighed myself down with obligation and responsibility and mortgages and all sorts of heaviness that would have kept us from taking flight.

I found myself actually grateful that the life I thought I wanted hadn't worked out for me, because I got to find something even better. It was so simple to pack up our two-bedroom apartment and live flexibly. It was so simple it felt almost dangerous and wrong.

Why is it normal to weigh ourselves down with accumulation and responsibility?

Why do we want more of this *perception* of success when it actually *limits* our choices to procure it, and then sustain it?

Most of us don't really want *more*—we want the freedom that a life like that seems to represent. We want the *feeling* of it, but not the actual logistics of it. It's a lot of responsibility to own multiple homes, to have hundreds of people rely on you for their livelihood, to sustain fame, to manage staff, to deal with the logistics of a life that complex. Maybe what we crave isn't the conventional success, but what we've been told you get to feel at that level—who you get to be and what possibilities open for you.

Accolades and impressive achievements feel sexy and do get lots of attention from people. It's an unfortunate thing, because so much of what is impressive and glitzy can be fabricated. Followers can be bought on social media. Press placements are now overwhelmingly paid for. Investor capital looks tantalizing and impressive but often it means loss of control of what you've built. A "perfect" life might be overridden with debt. The perfect house looks so good on an Instagram post but on month nineteen of overstretching to afford it, does it feel as good?

It takes a significant amount of self-exploration and honesty to admit that certain things you want are so you can say you have them to people who mostly don't care. People care, but people care about their own life. Hustling to try to impress them might be temporarily rewarded, but it's ultimately an empty result.

If you're not doing something for you, why do it?

Our society has created an allure around being liked by others. But really, how your life looks to others doesn't matter. What matters is how it *feels*. How it feels to *you*. The success of your life is how happy, joyful, and free you are on a daily basis, how true it feels to you, how fulfilling you find it. You're the only one living your life, after all. And often the thing that you think will make your life *look* impressive hardly ever *feels* the way you want it to.

So, what if your happiest life wasn't going to be very impressive by societal standards? Would you still want it? Or are you still wanting the rewards of societal acceptance more?

Maybe you don't want to climb the corporate ladder. Or be a millionaire. Or live to work. Maybe you want to opt out of the whole system. Do you notice the tension in your body, the worry of "what people will think?" It's normal. We've been conditioned to care. But it's a trap.

You're not broken. You don't need to be fixed. You are not a perpetual self-improvement project.

Grow, yes. Learn, definitely. Stretch yourself, absolutely. But do it from a place of foundational happiness. Get to the feelings first.

The conventions do not serve us. Their definitions are so narrow.

You are so much more than these definitions, than these conventions. You cannot be contained. Don't let them limit you. Be wide, open, expanded—take up all the space in your own life.

CHAPTER 3

I'll Be Happy When . . .

LEARNING HOW TO BE HAPPY not when, but *now*—is the real work of a life. Not when it all lines up, but right now, in the messiness of being alive.

Because even when it does seem to all line up, you're still you. Most people get to the moment they've been waiting for—they've checked off all their boxes and they expect the happiness to flood right in. And when it doesn't, because they haven't done the work internally, they just make a new milestone. They say, okay, then I'll be happy when *this* elevated thing happens. I'll be happy in the bigger house, in the nicer clothes, in the better car.

But the work of being happy is not an accumulation. It's not an eventuality after you've achieved enough and own enough and have enough. Think of how wildly unfair that would be in a world that is so deeply inequitable. If happiness were only for the people in the biggest houses with the dreamiest and most impressive jobs, then what about all the people who have no access to this kind of opportunity? Do they not deserve happiness?

It's a privilege malaise, to believe happiness is in accumulation. And so many of us are convinced that we'll be happy when some achievement is met, when a milestone is reached, when we hit the pinnacle of our careers, when when when. We're completely ignoring that the most important opportunity of our lives is right in front of us, waiting to be noticed: finding a way to be happy right here, right now, exactly rooted in what our life currently is.

No *when*. No *if*.

Once you take the "when" and "if" out of the equation, you can clearly see which dreams stay, which dreams go, and what's next.

The "when" actually blocks our potential.

As a girl, I'd often escape into my daydreams. During boring moments or when I was trying to sleep, I'd concoct new realities for myself. At first, it was harmless. But then, as I grew up and entered my teens and then my twenties, it became a way to disassociate from reality. It became a way to leave myself and imagine a new life that felt increasingly far away.

It became a way for me to escape into "I'll be happy when . . ."

I'll be happy when I've lost weight.

I'll be happy when this guy likes me.

I'll be happy when I've achieved this thing.

What started as a harmless way to flex my imagination became something that actively harmed me, a place I could go to escape myself and the present moment.

When I made the decision to change my life and find happiness right where I was, I knew I had to let go of the daydreams. I was still using that as a place to retreat to, a place to perfect my life. I'd lull myself to sleep with these fantasies, and of course the life I'd constructed in my mind wasn't messy or difficult or anxiety-ridden. No, it was always perfect. And so, reality felt like a lackluster version of the life I was living inside my mind. I wouldn't allow myself to be happy until I had all of the things I was dreaming about, thinking that it was my motivation. Not being happy was my punishment for not being *there* yet.

And I was missing my real, imperfect, beautiful life by escaping there.

Letting go of the perfect picture I had of my life felt like killing off a part of myself. Achievement isn't bad on its own. Achievement can be wonderful. But achieving when you are truly able to embrace it from a healed place is one thing. Achieving when you are trying to prove your worth—it complicates everything.

But, I didn't know what I was going to look forward to. I remember thinking to myself: So without my "I'll be happy when's" I just have . . . Right Now? I hate my Right Now! Nothing is okay in my Right Now! My Right Now isn't perfect at all—I'm not anywhere I expected to be and I'm not thin and I'm not accomplished enough and my marriage takes work and I'm not a famous writer—I'm nothing. I felt as if I was nothing, with proof. I felt I had nothing.

Which, of course, wasn't true, but escaping into the "I'll be happy when . . ." had made it true.

Because it's all completely perfect in our minds. There are never any obstacles or fear or anxiety or fights or insecurities when we play it out in our minds.

When I stopped my daydreams, when I stopped projecting my happiness onto some future moment of perfection, I watched as several dreams fell away. Once I realized that I couldn't really achieve my way into a certain kind of contentment, I had to root myself in the present over and over, and find that contentment exactly where I was. I had to be radically present. Radically content. Radically honest. Anything else wasn't going to work.

The achievements, the accomplishments, the milestones— they went to their rightful place: as the additions to an already beautiful life in progress. Not when. Not if. Now.

I realized, on this journey, that what I had assumed was "happiness" was not that at all.

It was healing.

Wholeness.

Peace within.

Emotional harmony.

I realized that my fantasies and disassociations had become a way to escape into a healed version of myself.

I realized how much time I'd spent on the sidelines, watching other people enjoy their lives, caved in on myself. How much of my life I'd spent feeling undeserving, unworthy, and hesitant. How I let the world tell me who I am, where I belong, and what experiences I get to have. How many times I put my joy on layaway until I was "better."

By letting go of the "I'll be happy when . . . " mentality, I was able to work on healing myself and how I saw myself. I was able to appreciate who I was in the present. I refused to let another moment pass me by. I refused to be a sideline character in my own existence.

It wasn't that I had become so undeniably happy that I never had a bad day or a difficult situation or an unruly mood. It's that I had healed enough to know I could handle any life situation that came up unexpectedly. I healed so that I could actually hear my emotions, instead of denying and repressing them, terrified of what they might reveal to me.

I thought it was happiness I was longing for, but it turned out that what I wanted more than anything was the healing. It's in that healing that I was able to notice the moments of my life that were beautiful, or challenging, or opportunities to evolve even deeper.

It doesn't matter where we go, what we achieve, or how much we change our external life. The one constant is how we feel about ourselves, how much we allow ourselves to feel, how much of our past we heal and evolve from. I've been deeply unhappy in lots of beautiful places. Wherever you go, there you are.

I spent so much of my teens and twenties afraid to face myself. Because of that, I'd escape into those fantasies, thinking that I would be happy once I checked off all these life achievements. I was terrified of my emotions, of what they'd reveal to me if I felt them, if I looked at them, if I spent considerable time with myself, without distracting, avoiding, numbing, disassociating, and escaping. I drank a lot of alcohol to avoid that reckoning. I smoked a solid amount of weed to avoid it. I overate to avoid it. I was reckless and obsessive with men and women to avoid it. I spent my twenties constructing a mechanism within that would do anything and everything I could to avoid the healing I needed the most. I don't remember being nineteen years old. Or twenty-two. Or twenty-four. I wasn't present. Alive. I was operating from my most unhealed, fearful self, terrified that if I slowed down, if I faced myself, if I opened myself up to that kind of vulnerability—that I'd fall apart.

But, I've come to understand that sometimes you need to fall apart, so you can reconstruct yourself in a stronger way.

I assumed that if I could become this accomplished woman,

then I wouldn't have to face my own reckoning. I thought I could bypass the healing. If I could just do enough, become enough, then I wouldn't have to face my trauma, or my misgivings, or my past pain. I wouldn't have to look at how I treat myself or how this world has conditioned me to be. It wasn't rational. It was based in fantasy, where rules or realities don't apply.

In that world, I wouldn't have to heal.

The achievements would heal me. The right partner would heal me. The weight loss would heal me. If I could just become the perfect version of myself, then I wouldn't have to look at the imperfect, unhealed, flawed, pained, hurting parts of myself.

I could finally prove I was good enough, that I was lovable, that I was admired, that I was all the things I was scared I wasn't. I didn't want to find out that maybe deep down I wasn't worthy of love, so if I could just gather up enough evidence to prove it all to myself, then I'd be okay.

And yet, the solution was always a lot simpler than this.

The solution wasn't to keep achieving, accumulating, formulating evidence.

The solution came in the healing.

I had to slow everything down, and face myself.

When Houssem and I got to France in 2018, I took hundreds of pictures of him. He grew up without cameras, so he makes up for lost time by wanting a picture for every single activity we do, no matter how mundane. My camera roll was filled with pictures of him. Even when we met in 2011 and spent the year in Paris and then in Berlin—every picture is of him. I didn't want to have my picture taken. More accurately, I didn't think I was *worth* having my picture taken. Because of that, I am mostly absent from the first few years we spent together. I cried before my wedding day, not wanting to have my arms exposed in my dress. I was about to be married, and all I could fixate on was whether my arms were going to be too "fat" in the pictures.

I used to have to brace myself before looking at a picture of myself, knowing I'd find a relentless amount of flaws in it. My stomach would drop when looking at myself. I wouldn't think of the memory, or the moment, or anything else except—look at the way my stomach is, look at my arms, look at my face. The anguish at my own body was present in the energy of the photo, too. I looked as uncomfortable as I felt.

I spent a lot of time waiting for permission to be visible in my own life.

Pictures can seem like a weird segue into this lesson for me, but those pictures represented so much more than vanity. Pictures are declarations of worth. Maybe for some people it's vanity, but for so many others, especially women, we hold ourselves hostage to the moment. If we can't let go and capture our life in a picture, what else are we grasping? What else are we hiding from?

I hid so often, and so much. If ever there was a picture of me, it was a head in the background of a group shot. And I remember feeling hidden away in those moments, too. The picture reflected the reality. The more I hid away from pictures, the more I hid away from life. It was all connected.

In France in 2018, I was having a body revolution. It was a

master class in confidence, especially in Paris. I had to force myself to feel good about myself at first. The Parisiennes can be so body-obsessed. They are not shy about looking you up and down on the Metro, examining you, approving or disapproving of you. The French are wonderful, but they do not have the overt politeness of Americans. They are truthful, and sometimes even the way they look at you without a word spoken can feel harsh. At first, I felt exposed. And then, it became the most freeing thing—their looks, their gruffness.

I remember being in Paris in April 2018, and I had to make a decision. I felt a little on edge, shaky with my confidence. I'd done a lot of self-love work the year before, but this was the practical application of it. Would I lose myself and what I'd built in Paris? Could I hold on to myself through this? I felt the grasp of my confidence loosening.

But then I realized I only had two real choices: I could let my self-esteem go up and down with the perceived approval or disapproval of the many strangers I was coming in contact with on a daily basis, or I could like my body exactly the way it is and just be free. I could wait for permission from all these strangers, never fully grasping it because how do you get permission from people you never meet or talk to? I could let the opinion I perceived they had of me determine how I was going to enjoy this precious time in a beautiful city—or I could just . . . stop caring what they thought.

It was revolutionary.

I could just *not* wait for permission.

I could stop saying to myself: I'll be happy when . . .

I'll enjoy this when . . . I'm thinner.

Instead, I could completely and radically opt out of their opinion.

I could approve of myself unconditionally, instead of waiting for it from someone else, from faceless majorities, from strangers I assumed were making judgments about me. Even if they judged, why did I need to care? I only cared because other people's opinions were more important to me, but if their opinions didn't have importance to me—I would stop caring. This seemed too obvious. And yet, it has become the basis of my life now. I simply just do not care that much how other people perceive me.

I'd rather just . . . live freely.

And stop buying into the pervasive idea that I don't get to decide who I am, what I am worthy of, what is valuable about me, and forget everyone else.

This blew my mind.

It felt like I had stumbled on a piece of rare and precious information.

I could just walk around Paris and not care at all what anyone thought of me. The pieces of me I was handing out to everyone else, searching for their approval, could all come back to me. I did not need to care whether some random French person on the Metro thought poorly of me.

What could their opinion do to me? I was making their opinions mean something. I was giving everyone else's opinion of me higher importance than my own. It didn't really matter what I thought about myself. It only mattered what other people thought of me. It seemed ridiculous when I pointed it out to myself, when I had the revelation, but then I realized—I've been thinking like this my entire life. And I know many other people who think like this, too.

Because, as a woman especially, we are taught to be in service of others. We are taught to derive value in how *others* perceive us. Are we good enough? Are we pretty enough? Are we doing enough? How are we doing? Tell us how we're doing!

But, my life is not a focus group.

And, I was done. I was done trying to get enough permission to be worthy of my own existence. I was done deriving value for myself by how much approval I could attain from others. I was done letting my body—and other people's judgments of my body— keep me from the experience I was having. I was in Paris! And I was going to let other people rob me of the joy of my own life?

That first revolutionary step led to even more confidence. It generated a well of it. I felt bolstered by it. I didn't have to wait any longer. I could walk around the streets of Paris in my "imperfect" body, in clothes that did not have a size S on the label, within a life that wasn't perfect by any means—and still feel the most joy, excitement, wonderment, and awe. The Seine didn't care whether my arms were toned—the water glittered and I stopped to take it in. The Eiffel Tower lit up every thirty minutes and I was still able to feel the unbridled wonder of it, even if my body wasn't thin and lithe, even if I wasn't in the exact career I had dreamed of having, even if nothing at all was lined up yet.

Everything about those four months in Paris felt urgent. I showed up as the most healed, free version of myself. And I've continued to free myself more, peel back more layers, evolve and change from that place. Houssem took so many pictures of me in Paris, and my camera roll filled up with smiles. The more I saw myself in my life, the more I became someone worthy in my life.

It's strange that the pictures held so much significance.

But, I've come to understand that pictures are a witness to life. And I deserve to be in the forefront of my own life. I deserve to be the main character in the story of my life. I deserve to put myself first. I deserve to be seen. And I deserve to be seen in whatever iteration of my body I'm in. I deserve to have my moments captured.

Not when. Not if. Not someday. Not when I'm finally "perfect," whatever that means.

I don't have to look a certain way, or have a certain amount of money, or have a certain kind of job, or be a certain kind of person—I am allowed to be seen exactly as I am. I do not and should not wait for permission for that. This is my life. Mine. I'm allowed to exist fully within it.

Realizing that I did not need to wait for permission to be acceptable, accepted, or approved of in order to live the life I most desired—it felt like a radical change. Something that simple, and yet we are told over and over how much our worth is out there, somewhere, in the hands of others. When I got off that hierarchy, stopped playing that game, it felt that my life was able to blossom and change in all the ways I'd been craving.

Coming back to LA in 2019 and moving to Calabasas in that mind-set, in that space—I was able to better create the life I wanted. Not the life I thought would be impressive, but the life that felt wonderful to me. Nothing is off-limits. I don't have to wait. I'm allowed to have the life I desire right here. I may not get everything I want, but even that I welcome. It wasn't meant for me. I want to be in alignment with what is meant for me. Whatever happens, I will love that.

I believe so much of the pain in this world is caused by unhealed people. I know I caused pain to others and to myself from that unhealed place. There's so much trauma inflicted on others by people who refuse to reckon with themselves, who refuse to take responsibility for their own healing, who think they can achieve their way into feeling whole. The grasp for power is a way to bypass healing. The greed, the accumulation, the over emphasis on superficial achievements—it's all a way to get around the healing.

Because healing is a torrential process. Anyone who has decided to reckon with themselves knows that it's not all bubble baths and face masks. Everything you've spent years avoiding now has to come to the surface. Not everybody welcomes that. And yet, it's essential. It's not possible to experience true joy, happiness, peace, harmony, and love without healing through the parts of you that believe you don't deserve those things. Healing from the past traumas that make it difficult to even notice your life when you're in it. Without healing, there is only the suppression or repression of emotions.

Healing is the freedom that so many of us have tried to achieve our way into.

When I started this whole journey, I felt terrified of my emotions. I didn't want to look into them, never mind actually *feel* them. And then it felt like I vacillated to the extreme, where I *only* wanted to feel happiness. I started to realize that the healed state is being in the middle of it all. Expecting to never have a "negative" emotion ever again is impossible. No matter how much you achieve, how much money you have, whatever your life situation—those emotions will come up. Life happens. Staying in a "good vibes only" state is impossible. And that's okay.

Happiness is only part of the whole. Healing and continuing to heal means accepting and feeling *all of it*. Not expecting perfection, or only "good" vibes, or only "positive" experiences. These things are out of our control. It's what we do with the uncertainty that creates the well-being.

When we are no longer terrified of failure, rejection, disappointment, sadness, grief, any of it—that's when we're on the path to healing.

When you can feel these things, learn from them, deepen your relationship to yourself and others through them—that, to me, is being in a healed state. Happiness can come and go. Joy can be experienced in lots of moments. There is pleasure to be had. There is jubilation and excitement. These are heightened states. But the calm contentment that we crave is about being healed. Letting what happens, happen, and knowing that you are always at home with yourself, that you can always heal through anything that comes up.

A healed mind doesn't need to create stories about your worthiness or deservedness when something "negative" happens. A rejection means a redirection. A disappointment is something that was meant to miss you. You can be aligned with what's meant for you when you are healed. When you can safely feel your emotions.

It's about healing and alignment. Don't disassociate. Reckon with yourself. Tell the truth to yourself. When a trickier emotion rises to the surface, the best thing you can do is listen to it, try to understand the wisdom in it, and sit with it. Try not to suppress, distract, and numb the harder emotions. Don't play the "I'll be happy when . . . " game to avoid the healing. It's a distraction. Your life is here. Right now. Not when.

Don't be afraid of your own healing. Welcome it. When something triggers you, find a way to connect to yourself. And when something misses you, don't cling to it. What's meant for you, will be.

And whenever that inner peace becomes harder to grasp, your work is not to complete more tasks, to achieve more, to try to change some external circumstance to feel a certain way. It's a call for healing. Because, that's the thing, too. Healing is an unpeeling. It's like an onion. There are ever more layers.

And isn't that what we're here to do?

To peel it all back and get to something real and true within.

To find love within.

To be able to heal and gently share that healing with others.

To heal toward a more beautiful, equitable, and loving world.

Starting within us first.

CHAPTER 4

I Can Never Settle

YOU DON'T HAVE TO go live off the grid to find simplicity. You don't have to stop wanting big things in order to feel satisfied. You don't have to stop *dreaming*.

That's the overriding tenet of being radically content.

Your life needs to be for you. It needs to be *your* version of dreaming. Your version of health. Your version of a beautiful life. That kind of thing isn't prescriptive. I can't tell you what it looks like for you. I can't tell you what your truth is.

You deserve to enjoy your life.

We can have it all, but do we want it all? That's the real question.

What is enough?

When are we settling and when are we fulfilled? How do we even know?

We have become a generation obsessed with never "settling." It's an amorphous thing, ever-changing, ever-mutable—*settling*. There is no definition for it. What does it look like to settle? Is it the fenced-in yard and a house in the suburbs? To some, that's a nearly impossible dream. Someone's most "settled" life could be someone else's dream life.

So, we are scared of doing a thing that can't be defined.

Throughout my twenties, the idea of "settling" plagued me. Nothing ever felt good enough. I had a difficult time committing— to myself, to others, to projects, to friendships, to relationships, to a college major, to a field of study, to a career, to a place to live. The grass seemed to always be greener somewhere else. And I thought obsessively about whether the more comfortable I got, the more I was settling. Society tells us your "best life" is always out of your comfort zone, but sometimes I just wanted to breathe. Yet, in those moments of exhale, I'd panic. I'm *settling*. I need to push. I need to keep grinding. To rest, to relax, to even stop worrying about my future—it all felt like giving up.

I was so scared of ever settling that I never committed to *settling in*. I never stayed consistent. My past was a graveyard of good intentions.

I was so concerned with always living my absolute "best life" that I didn't spend time building a good life at all. I was living under the belief that, at any given moment, I was falling behind. The race for achievement, to never settle, to always be pushing— it felt urgent. Like I only had a decade—my twenties—to get it all perfect. Otherwise, by thirty, it would be over. If you haven't "made it" by thirty, you're a "late bloomer." I thought thirty was so old, until I turned thirty and realized it was so young.

But this urgency of "falling behind" followed me around throughout my teens and twenties. I never felt like I was on the trajectory I "should" be on. I didn't date when my friends did. I was shy and scared of rejection. I felt like the world seemed to go on without me, leaving me behind. That was a pervasive feeling for me as a teenager: feeling left behind.

And so I became a woman in her twenties trying to catch up.

Trying not to ever settle.

Trying to prove that there was nothing "wrong" with me for being left behind the way I felt I was.

I was buying into the incorrect belief that anything after thirty isn't impressive or is too late.

Now, I'm thirty-six and feel like I'm in some wild place of possibility. Like I've burned through all these limiting beliefs and get to just live the way I want to live.

When we internalize societal expectations and take them on as our own, we are conforming. We may not define it that way, but that's what it is. And at some point in my early thirties, I decided not to conform. I refused to let my life be dictated by these narrow beliefs about what women get to do at what age. I refused to believe that I'd hit some cutoff and that my value and worth would decline with each passing year after thirty. It's a lie. If the external world wasn't going to affirm me, then I would be intent on affirming myself. At every age.

I resent the idea of late bloomers. It might seem like a compliment. It might be a way to assuage the feeling that coming into your dreams later could be a positive thing. But in actuality it creates a time line, where no time line needs to exist. There is no time line for blooming. Who decides when a person is "late"? Can we ever really be "late" to our own lives?

We can all bloom at our own pace, thank you very much.

I decided after the chaos of turning thirty that I'd never let my age determine my possibilities ever again. I'd stop being so worried about "settling" and, instead, learn to enjoy my life at every stage I was in, every version of myself I'd become, every old skin I'd shed. And instead of having my life be a fear of settling, I'd simply live as wholly and honestly as I could and continue to grow and evolve as needed.

That's the thing about settling—and our fixation on it. We

forget that if we are always afraid of settling, then that means we're never settling *in*. It's very hard to build the kind of life we want, one that feels worn and comfortable, if we are looking out at the horizon, thinking there *could* be something better. I love to challenge myself. I love to find new dreams. I love to achieve. I love to think big. But I don't want to do all that while also feeling constantly unsettled in my everyday life. That tension—of loving where you are and building where you're going—is one of the most important things for me to balance.

Since "settling" has no definition and is entirely subjective, I've tried to understand what it is we are attributing to a life where someone settles. Settling is not a place or a configuration of a life. It's a feeling. And I've come to realize that when we have unspent dreams within us, when we aren't living honestly to our truest selves, when we are hiding parts of ourselves away, when we are neglecting to honor our deepest desires—that is a life that feels like settling. And that kind of life can look like anything at all. Someone can live inauthentically in a beautiful beach house in Malibu, while someone else can be living to their truest self in a van on the side of the Pacific Coast Highway.

Where I think we get it wrong is when we ascribe a definition to settling that is based on someone else's life. And instead of living based on what feels most true to us, we think not-settling is simply acquiring what that other person has. The keeping up. The falling behind. The aging out of dreams. It's all based on other people's definitions. And when we use other people's definitions, we are taken directly out of our own life, our own truth.

When we are following someone else's map, even if we line it all up perfectly, it's going to feel like we've settled because we haven't lived in our own truth. What looks like big dreams to me might be small dreams to someone else. What feels expansive to me might feel constricting to another person. What felt expansive to me two years ago now feels constricting.

But if we use strict definitions of what it looks like to "settle" and follow the "shoulds" that are lobbed at us all the time, then we are missing the most important information: the kind of life that would make each of us our happiest, most fully expressed self. And that is meant to look different from your neighbor, your parents, your siblings, your friends. It's not supposed to follow a carbon copy superimposed on your own life. It's meant to be yours.

I think when we are afraid of settling, what we're really afraid of is not being radically honest about what we most want. We're afraid of not going after the dreams we haven't yet admitted out loud. We're afraid that if we try, we'll fail. Or, worse, if we try, we may succeed—and it'll upset the carefully constructed identity we've created. We're afraid of stepping outside the bounds of those societal "shoulds" and living in our own definitions of what our most free life really is. We're afraid of throwing the whole map out and setting off to explore without it.

Because society does give a map. A friend group gives a map. Parents can give a map. Everyone is trying to give a map. But if you don't create your own map, you'll follow someone else's path. Maybe it will make you happy. Most likely, it won't. And when you follow that map, when you get all the things you thought you were supposed to have, when you fulfill *their* dreams and needs, when you sit there surrounded by the life that was supposed to make you happy—*that* can feel like settling. That can feel like a prison. That can feel so disillusioning it brings you to your knees.

But other people don't have to live your life, so why do they get to give you a map?

And why do we let them?

The life you most want is the one you *decide* on, the map you write for yourself. It might not be as easy as following a prescribed route, but it will be a lot more fun—and it will feel like *your* life.

I think we rush through that part. We think we have to figure out our entire lives in our twenties and then settle right down in our thirties. We have *one* decade to determine how we'll live for the next five, six, seven decades of our expected life span. And we completely normalize this.

We really do think of thirty as a checkpoint.

You have to get it all accumulated—the perfect person, the perfect career, the one place you'll live forever, the friendships, the life—and then you just have to live it, never changing, never growing.

That's the line we've been fed.

That's the expectation.

That you turn thirty and your possibilities for growth, change, excitement, fun, joy, love, new directions, new versions of yourself—it's over. Which is also why we have people who are frantic to figure it all out in their twenties, growing up too fast, taking on responsibilities too soon, making permanent decisions that their older selves may not line up with.

They are trying so hard to get it all perfect before they turn thirty that they don't even stop themselves to ask what they want, what they really, truly, deeply *want*. They are so busy following the societal map that they may wake up one day in a life that doesn't even feel like it belongs to them.

I know that's how I was in my twenties. I know that when I hit thirty, the expectations leveled me. I know that I felt as if my life was about to get worse, that I was on a downhill. I know that every internalized panic came to the surface, and I felt that my life was essentially over, that I'd never get to dream again, that I wasn't good enough because I couldn't get it all figured out before that age.

If I was that *openly* frantic when I turned thirty, I can only imagine the *latent* panic that lived in my body before it came to the surface. There are many decisions I made in my twenties out of fear of turning thirty without figuring it all out. There were many opportunities I probably should have turned down, but felt I had to take them on because I only had a couple of years to "make it."

But what if we thought of aging as a gift, and not as a fixed determination of what's possible? That there's always ample room to grow and shift and change. I hope to become many versions of myself. I already have. I have allowed myself to take on new identities, to try on life experiences as if they are new clothes. I look forward to all the many women I get to become in my future, all the versions of myself I will evolve into and outgrow.

Outside the bounds of the "shoulds" is a beautiful life that isn't filled with societal pressure.

That's where I live now.

The visual I have in my mind is me, floating in some space-like place, and the chaos of the world is something I can only observe. I'm not saying I don't get affected by societal pressures, but I can identify them now, without playing into them. I don't want a life that looks like everybody else's. I don't want to be limited by what society tells me is or is not possible.

Settling, to me, feels like ignoring my gifts. It feels like telling myself something isn't possible when I haven't even tried. It feels like saying I'm too old to do what I want to do. It feels like rejecting myself before someone else might reject me. It feels like avoiding the hard work of believing in myself so that I never get disappointed. It feels like waiting for someone else to affirm or validate me. It feels like living a life that I know is more constricted than I am capable of. It feels like ignoring that quiet, still voice within me that says I am meant for more than this.

That doesn't mean I *want* more. Or that I am more valuable with more. It has nothing to do with consumption. It has everything to do with me continuing to grow and evolve—and not let myself get stuck in the muck of what this narrow-minded society tells me is possible for a woman who is my size, age, socioeconomic status, etcetera.

I'm not going to let other people determine the life I should have in order to justify the life they've decided on—and neither should you. I am going to do the work of healing and evolving into new levels of myself. I am going to honor the gifts and talents I've been given. The very least I can do is express those gifts and talents.

My age does not determine where I go or when I give up. Age can't tell me anything except how long I've had the privilege to be on this Earth. I never want to see another woman cut her potential off at the helm, simply because she thinks she's aged out of her opportunities. Simply because this society has told her that her value plummets after thirty.

I will not let society tell me what my value is. I don't care. They can ascribe all their definitions and values to me, but it doesn't stick. I set the value. I set my worth. I determine my possibilities. Everyone else will just have to rise to my level. That's not arrogance. It's confidence. It's beyond the bounds of what society has tried to drill into me my entire life: Who gets a voice. Who gets to be valuable at what age. How my life should look. How I should look.

I don't listen anymore. I just shrug at the noise. I hear it. I recognize it. I can understand it's there. But I have free will on whether I will listen.

Those limits aren't serving me. And they aren't serving you either. There is so much to be experienced beyond thirty, beyond any age. So much life to live. So much more out there for you to discover about the world and about yourself. Don't cut that off. And don't weigh yourself down with so much expectations that you have no room to grow, or evolve, or shake it all off to become someone else entirely.

We are meant to bloom. We are meant to change shape. We are meant to live to the fullest extent. We are meant to have the gifts and joys and abilities and interests that we have. Those are for us. They are called *gifts* for a reason. And they don't exist just for everyone else to enjoy. You are *allowed* to enjoy your gifts.

Stop worrying so much about "settling" and start asking yourself whether you're living the way *you* most want to. Are you drawing your own map? Are you forging your own path? Are you clear on what you most desire? Are you letting your dreams become known? Are you giving yourself space and time to enjoy the process of realizing those dreams? Are you living based on your own definitions?

Stop worrying about getting it all right for everyone else, and think about getting it right within. Get your soul in harmony. Keep your own promises.

And live outside the bounds of society, of conformity, of the status quo. You are meant for so much more than those small boxes. You are meant to live in a way that truly and unabashedly lights you up. That's not going to look like anyone else's life—and that is the magic of it.

If you can get there—and stay there—in the place where you are living based on your own map, the worry of "settling" will completely go away. You won't even think of it any longer. It will be like a distant dream.

Because when you are living for you, outside the bounds, opting out of what society says you should do, then you have no need or desire to measure up. There's no one to measure up to.

It's only past you, present you, and future you.

Take all the pieces of your worth and bring them back home. Affirm yourself. Value yourself. If there's anything you're doing to try to prove how good you are at being good, become aware of it and stop doing it. Heal from it. Bring it all back inside. That belongs to you. That's your job. How other people think of you is on them. How you think of you is what matters—that is *your* job.

From that point, see what you still want to do in your life. See which dreams stay and which ones go.

You may be surprised.

You may unlock a magic within you that you didn't think you had.

You may be set on a path that is better and brighter and more you than where you thought you'd be heading.

You may just find that life unfolds for you beautifully when you stop hustling so hard for your worth. Life may just rise to the level you've set when you know how worthy you are, right here, right now.

CHAPTER 5

I'm My Own Worst Enemy (and So Is Everyone Else)

WE ARE DEEPLY UNKIND to ourselves. For many, being inside our own mind is the harshest place to be. We speak to ourselves with such a stunning lack of compassion. We'd never speak to a friend in that way, but somehow we've accepted that being our own worst enemies is totally normal: We *should* be hard on ourselves. We *should* always be pushing and striving. We should *never* become complacent. We should be *vigilant* with ourselves. How else will we achieve all the things we're "supposed" to achieve if we're not cruel to ourselves? That's giving up! *Right?*

If your mind is a battlefield, like mine was for so many years, I understand. But here's the thing: It's not natural for us to be our own worst enemy. We do not have to accept that being hard on ourselves is the normal way. Or that being hard on ourselves actually creates a happy life. It might create a panicked, over-productive life. It may look impressive to the external world, because you never give up, never quit, and are always grinding yourself down to who the world expects you to be. Is it the most prevalent way to live? Yes, definitely. But just because something is normalized does not mean it's *best* for us.

We cause a lot of wreckage in our lives in order to avoid our emotions. In order to avoid what we are being called to face. We create stories about what's possible for us. We believe the most negative things about us are the most true. We do not expect to have kindness in our minds.

Some of us are deeply in pain from how harsh we are to ourselves, because we've normalized that our inner world should be turmoil. That there's no other way. And most of us don't realize that we have come to identify with the strict stories in our mind as some sort of irrefutable truth. As if our identities are fixed. As if we can't rewrite or edit our stories.

The problem is, when we have the harshness inside our minds, we look for solutions outside of us. We want to prove our own minds wrong. We try to achieve our way into confidence. We try to sleep with or marry our way into loving ourselves. We try to accumulate enough accolades that our worthiness will be inevitable. We try to do enough and impress enough people to finally be able to say: Okay, *now* I'm good enough. And we try to make it all a lot harder than it needs to be so that we can *deserve* it. We berate ourselves in some wild, misunderstood hope that it will create the content life we crave.

There's no oasis where pain or insecurity cease to exist once you've lined everything up. That doesn't happen. There are plenty of people at the top of whatever mountain you're scaling who are not happy. Conventional success amplifies how we truly feel inside. And if we have been hustling in order to prove our minds wrong, then that becomes how we experience any success as well. It becomes more hustle. More striving. The next milestone. I'll feel like I deserve it when I get *there*. And *there* becomes a moving target that never, ever can be hit.

Most people feel like failures if they haven't hit certain milestones by certain ages. That's the way of our society. The media is obsessed with youthful achievement, making those achievements mean that happiness is inevitable for those people. This is not true. It's not even kind of true. It's simply a lie.

And it's a lie that keeps a lot of us feeling like failures, feeling like we're behind, feeling like we get to a certain age and we must give up. It keeps us thinking that our sense of worth is out there, somewhere, waiting to be earned.

We cannot earn our worth.

Let's read that again.

We cannot earn our worth.

You cannot earn your worth.

In 2016, I started journaling, and for the first time in my life, I was doing something consistently. That year of journaling felt like an exorcism. It was deeply uncomfortable. Unhealed parts of me would lash out on the page. Unfiltered thoughts would wound me. It became clear very quickly that I did not like myself. That I was, without a doubt, my own worst enemy. Whatever anyone had said to me in the past, whatever hurtful thing I'd endured, I'd internalized it and amplified it and regurgitated something even worse.

I knew I was hard on myself, that I had high expectations, that I was a "perfectionist," but journaling these thoughts made me realize it was much more harmful than that. I was an abusive person to myself, and these were the thoughts running on repeat in my mind all day, every day. No wonder I wasn't able to access happiness or peace. I was creating chaos in my mind and expecting calm.

I thought I was confident. I thought I was kind. I thought I was compassionate. But in the depths, in the spiral of my pain, in the past I hadn't yet been able to process, I was a person I didn't enjoy.

I was jealous. I was comparing myself to anyone I assumed was better than me, trying to take away their successes to make my perceived failures sting less. I was vastly unkind to myself. All the thoughts I had been able to render into static in a busy, chaotic, and frantic life were brought to heel—and the process of having to face these thoughts broke me open.

I thought being hard on myself was legitimately the only way to be. The alternative would be complacency, giving up on my life, like the drill sergeant in my mind was the one thing keeping me pushing and striving.

I accepted this voice in my head and made a sort of twisted peace with it. This was the voice that was going to push me to finally prove everyone wrong. This was the voice that was going to make me "good enough." This was the voice that was going to keep me grinding and hustling for some vague future where all my insecurities would evaporate in the face of conventional success.

And this voice felt like the truth.

Compliments I received were lies—and the harsh voice in my head was the truth. And I wouldn't let go of the truth, because I thought I was the only one willing to say: *Jamie, you're not good enough yet.* I hadn't yet earned the right to be kind to myself. What would be my motivator if I wasn't using my own harshness against myself? How would I keep going?

That was the spiral I was in. Not for a day. Or a week. Or a month. But for two decades.

And that journal, pierced through with hard pen marks, became a salvation, a way to untangle all the many messages I'd been conditioned to believe about my worth, my place in the world, and what was required of me. Seeing my own cruel words on paper gave them a new shape, a new weight. It wasn't a funny meme. It wasn't a self-deprecating joke. I had to face the real cruelty of being my own worst enemy.

These words were creating my life.

These thoughts were telling me what was valuable about me.

And I felt overwhelmed by the tyranny of my own mind.

I kept needling to get to the root of it. Once I got beyond the initial shock of just how relentlessly unkind I was being to myself, I became almost addicted to pulling at the thread of every belief and story I could think of. It felt so good to get all this out in the open air. It felt like a release, a purification. I was finally looking at the parts of myself I had been desperate to hide, that I'd spent years avoiding with overeating, overdrinking, overconsuming. There was something cathartic about taking all of these thoughts I'd been terrified of and laying them out bare on the page. It was a sort of face-off—I see you now, and if I can name you, maybe you can't keep hurting me.

Once I excavated the stories I had about myself, the conditioning, the programming, I searched for roots. Getting to the root of a story, to me, is healing. What happened in my past and what did I make it mean? Because, it turns out, two people can have very similar experiences, but because of who they are and what came before or after that moment, they can make it mean two totally different things. Some people make rejection mean a redirect. And some people make rejection mean incontrovertible proof that they are not good enough. I was in search of what happened to me and what I made it mean.

There were reasons why I was so hard on myself, why my mind felt like a battlefield, why I didn't even feel safe within myself. It didn't just *happen*. There was societal conditioning, past trauma, and experiences that at the time I didn't know to let go of, but instead clenched them, created an entire identity around them, and made it all mean something more and bigger than it should have been.

I wasn't cool in high school. I wanted to be cool. I wanted to be friends with the popular kids. In class, we were all friends, but by the time the bell rang and we all dispersed, nobody grabbed my arm to bring me over to the cool table. I took this as rejection. I took this as proof that I wasn't good enough, that even though I was kind, and funny, and these same girls had been friends with me all through elementary and middle school, there was something flawed within me. I was second best, at best. I made this mean a lot of things, this core pain. Every time I interrogated the "good enough" narrative I had in my mind, high school would come up. The time when my best friends ditched me over the summer to start hanging out with a group of guys and I was left scrambling for a new group; that sinking feeling in my stomach at lunch time, wondering if I'd be accepted. All the times when the guy I liked so much would flirt with me mercilessly in class and then pretend I didn't exist outside in the corridors. The overarching pain of not being able to choose, but having my choices laid out for me already.

Just the pain of not being picked. Maybe I could have plucked up the courage to sit at the cool table, but the fact that I had no idea whether they'd want me there was the pain. That was the point.

And I made that mean a lot of things for a lot of years.

I made it mean that I was good, but not quite amazing, in my career. That I was a good writer, but nothing *special*. That I had to accept the mediocre friendships I had instead of set a standard for the friendships I really wanted. That no matter who I became out of high school, I could never outrun being the funny friend who nobody gave a second thought to once I was out of sight. I made it mean that I was not important, or meant for the kind of life I wanted, that I'd have to compromise continually. I made it mean that I couldn't declare what I wanted, because I'd never get it. Wanting had felt painful. Striving for something I couldn't have had burned like a fire within me.

I had so much to prove *wrong*.

That I wasn't the uncool high schooler who was terrified of sitting alone. That I had value. That I was chosen. That someone, anything, anyone—would choose me.

This all spilled out in the journal, in many ways creating a guide to myself. *This* led to *that*. Pull at this thread and this whole identity falls apart. Pull at this one and you get to the clarity. Match this story up with this root.

And then, I pulled *up* the roots.

I went even deeper in the journal and asked myself: Is this story really true? Is this one? This one? How about this one? And what stories were creating my reality?

Because if you think you don't deserve the life you want, I can tell you that taking the steps toward that life is nearly impossible. The deserving is not an outcome. It's a beginning. It's the only beginning.

I realized that I didn't have a "not doing enough" problem. I had a worth problem. A deserving problem. I was making that reality true over and over and over again. Even when I hit certain milestones, I was still making it true that it wasn't good enough. The thought was: If I got this—and I don't deserve to get what I want—then this isn't what I want. So, even if I was achieving so much—which I undoubtedly was at that point in my life—it was *still* not enough, because I believed at the core of myself that I didn't deserve to ever get what I wanted. Even when the blessings added up, it still didn't feel like enough. Because *I* didn't feel like enough.

It became clear that I could do anything and everything to try to earn my way into worthiness, but it wouldn't work. This was an inside job, an internal signal. I became almost thankful I hadn't received all that I thought I wanted, because if I didn't think I deserved it, then I probably would have self-sabotaged. I had self-sabotaged before on smaller scales. On a larger scale that self-sabotage can be catastrophic. I felt I had been spared that. And I started to sense a budding gratefulness for having been spared.

Seeing that I did not feel deserving or worthy of the life I thought I had been striving for in plain text, in my own hand, in the truth of an early morning light—I knew I had to find a new way. The old way was clearly not working. I'm the kind of person who can keep walking down the harmful path for a long time, but when I know better, I can't unknow it. That is a gift. Once the light goes on in the dark room, I can't unsee it. I have to change. I have to transform. I have to stay in the light of this new and valuable insight.

Clearing out the chaos in my mind through this journaling practice made me realize that I didn't have to be a relentless jerk to myself. I had to create a better way to exist in my own mind. I had seen the inside of me. I had crawled inside and held the parts of me that were in pain. I hadn't healed everything by any means, but I'd healed a deeper wound that I had been running away from for a long time. And every time I was unkind to myself, I felt the gash of it. It didn't sound like my normal voice any longer. It sounded like the ruthless voice that made my past pain mean I was unworthy of future joy. And I could not keep hurling that abuse at myself any longer. I simply couldn't.

Many of us spend decades creating chaotic lives to ultimately avoid that self-reckoning. We achieve and accumulate, thinking that if we get enough and become enough and impress enough that the need to heal those deep wounds will suddenly go away. As if we can earn our way out of our own reckoning.

But anyone who has done the deep healing knows that the reckoning always comes. It always finds a way to be expressed, whether it's conscious or not. Sometimes it means hurting other people. Sometimes it means hurting ourselves. But the wounds cannot go away. The harshness in our minds wants to be aired out. The healing wants to be felt.

You are not the one exception to the rule, thinking you can escape your healing and achieve your way into worthiness. If there is a wound within you telling you that you are not good enough, that you are not worthy, then that wound will get triggered at every single milestone. You've probably already experienced this happening, and instead of looking within to why that is, you maybe created a new milestone. A new goal. A new "when I get there, I'll feel better."

That dissatisfaction is not motivation.

It's a call for healing.

It's an invitation to pause and get deep within yourself. It feels like it's the trigger point to setting a higher goal, but in actuality it's a story within you that wants to be heard. It's a thread you are meant to pull on. It's a root that wants your attention.

You may be thinking no no no no no, I have to keep going, I have to keep achieving, I'm not *there* yet. You may think holding your own worth hostage until you've earned it is working for you.

But let me tell you something: When you access your worth without external conditions, that becomes a power and a magic that you cannot believe until you feel it. You think you're motivated now? You think you're doing a lot now? You think you're creative now?

Just wait until your skin isn't scratching for worth in every endeavor. Just wait until you know you are worthy right here, right now. Just wait when you are kind to yourself, when you can readily enjoy and accept and deserve your accomplishments. Just wait and see how beautiful your life can unfold when you already feel worthy, with or without achievement, or grand moments, or big houses, or big anything. Wait until the well of your creativity gets tapped not from trying to outrun your severe, exacting mind, but in celebration of how inspired you are. Wait until you create because you love to, not because you have to prove or strive or hustle.

Wait until your worth is conditional upon nothing at all.

You can be motivated by your own love, for the joy of it. For the experience. You don't need to be your own worst enemy in order to have a thriving life. Your mind can be a soft place to land for you. Your thoughts can be generative. It's not going to make you give up on life. It'll make you give up on the things that are draining you. And it'll give you back the things that light you up completely.

Do the deep healing. Pull at the threads.

Start interrogating that harsh voice in your head.

You don't have to be your own worst enemy.

You can, and must, be your own wonderful ally.

CHAPTER 6

Social Media Makes Me Feel Bad

I'VE COME TO UNDERSTAND that social media is a *reflection* of our current world. It can be a place of connection and learning, full of people you wouldn't otherwise meet. It can be a place that is wonderfully generative and eye-opening. Or, it can be a place you go to confirm all your worst fears about yourself—a place that inflames every last one of your insecurities, where you punish yourself for not yet "measuring up" to the ideals of the world.

There are highlight reels. There are people who are cashing in on aspirational lives, trading their followers' jealousy for paychecks. That exists. It will always exist. But as with anything else, your *intention* can change the experience of it. If you go on social media intending to follow and find people who will reflect unrealistic, disingenuous values, then that is absolutely what you will find. I used to do that. I used to go on social media in my most vulnerable moments, using it to punish myself for not being good enough yet. I thought it was "motivating." It was not.

Aspiration is not motivating. Let's unlearn that. You may think that exposing yourself to the perception of perfection will motivate you, but actually it can eat away at you and create insecurities where none existed before.

But if you use social media to confirm the kind of life you actually want, and align with people who make you feel capable, safe, and strong, then it can be the most beautiful place to spend time. The energy you give something is the energy you get back. If you approach social media wanting to learn and connect, you will find that. If you approach it with a punishing mind-set, you will find that.

And that's not just true about social media; it's true about life. This is a truth I've had to learn over and over, even recently.

I've had a week full of good news. It's a Saturday morning at the end of July. I don't typically write on the weekends, but I needed a lack of distractions today. I've just had a shower after breakfast, and in the shower, I felt a wave of insecurity hit me, an assault of it. That's how my insecurity hits me now. It used to be ubiquitous, like the moments of confidence were the outliers. I always noticed my confident moments. But now I can notice my insecure moments. I don't live there any longer. Insecurity visits me, but it doesn't stay. I've healed so much in order to be able to write that—and mean it.

While I ate my breakfast, I scrolled on Instagram. Off the heels of a celebratory week, I found myself scrolling profiles, feeling less and less confident and secure as I did so. I had hit a follower count milestone, and yet someone else whose work is similar to mine hit that milestone a year or more ago. Their last post got triple the likes of mine. No matter how many followers I get, someone else has more. No matter how much money I make, someone else is wealthier. No matter how much I progress, someone else has progressed so much further.

No matter what I have, someone has more.

On this particular morning, I feel pummeled by this. That no matter what I do, someone is doing it better, splashier, in ways that are more impressive.

I'm having a good year, but someone else—lots of someones— seems to be having a much better one. I got a book deal, but someone else got a seven-figure book deal. I was impressed with the amount I made with my digital course, but someone else is a multimillionaire from their courses. There are hundreds of women who don't have to write to garner millions of likes on their photos. There are TikTok *stars* already when I haven't even learned how to *use* TikTok, never mind become a star.

I'm doing well, but aren't there so many who are doing better?

And how can I ever expect to be satisfied when I have incontrovertible proof that their lives are better, more valuable, as defined by metrics and earning power?

I mean, more so, I don't even *deserve* to feel satisfied. If I feel satisfied, I'm accepting that I'm not ever going to be the best, that I won't dominate an industry, that I won't be able to use the comparisons in my favor. Look how much better I'm doing than all these other people. Compared to them, I'm killing it. There are plenty of people without book deals, without thousands of followers, without thousands of likes, without any passive income at all, *without without without.*

I can never ever be good enough, but maybe I'm better than someone else.

I negotiate with myself. Maybe I can be better than *this* group of people. Obviously, I'm doing better than *that* group. Not as good as *that* one. But I do have more than *that* person, and *those* people, too. And when I hit this next milestone, that'll be even more impressive. And I get to announce this thing, so that person I'm jealous of might then be jealous of me. And then maybe once I talk about this other thing, I'll be able to prove just how well I'm doing.

And then I get lost in this spiral, this negotiation of keeping up, this external reward and downgrading and upgrading—and I no longer know how I feel about anything. Just how *others* feel about everything.

And it happens in a snap.

In the shower on an ordinary Saturday, when I'm minding my own business, trying to wash the conditioner out of my hair. The wave of it, sudden. And at least now I'm in the place where I can notice it cresting over me. At least now I'm in the place where I can pull myself out of the riptide before I drown in it.

The wave of insecurity envelops me. And I try to talk it down. I try to negotiate with it, giving it proof that I am good enough. I stack up my achievements. I try to make myself better than the person I'm currently envious of. I feel like a lawyer. I'm trying to win the case of my adequacy. If I bring enough external evidence, maybe the jury will rule me Good Enough. If I get enough likes, enough followers, enough effusive messages dripping with praise, then I can compile it, label it, and use it in the case.

Suddenly, without even recognizing how I got here, I'm doing the proving thing again. I'm trying to collect enough approval and validation to tell the voice within me that says I'm *still* not good enough that actually I am. I'm trying to ease the pain in my chest with more and more. I'm trying to find fault with the other people who are doing "better" than me, so that I feel better for myself. I try to make it a Me vs. Them type of situation.

And what I'm doing is giving more power to this hypercompetitive, individualized culture I've grown up in. I'm fanning those flames. I am conforming more and more. I am becoming a part of the game.

Until I remind myself: I am trying to win an unwinnable game—again.

I am trying to win at a game that is *designed* to be unwinnable.

Social media is a microcosm of the world. That's what I've come to understand. People think there's an offline and an online self—as if they are not the same. They say online what they would never say offline, but that doesn't mean those thoughts and feelings don't exist somewhere. Social media just gives them an outlet, often a place to be anonymous. And yet, even in the anonymity, it gives a sense of what our culture cares about, what the value system is, and how people really feel about others, and, more so, how they feel about *themselves*. Whatever someone cruelly criticizes in another, they are criticizing within themselves. Intolerance and hatred start within. It's a poison.

And what I feel about social media, how that comparison makes me feel small and inadequate—that's how I feel offline, too. That's my conditioning, making itself known. That's me trying to win the game. That I am good if I am better than someone else. That all of life is a competition. That there are better and worse and good and bad and I just have to find out where I land. These are the binaries the world teaches us to live within. The metrics can feel definite. That it is value. But, it's only value if you conform to the ways of the world. If you don't challenge your own conditioning and socialization.

"Good enough" is another one of those vague concepts. Do

you see the pattern here—that all these things we strive for are nebulous and impossible to define? It's meant to be that way. If we can never see where the maze ends, we'll keep walking it, trying to win it, trying to figure it out, trying to do anything within our power to find an exit that doesn't exist.

The person I was comparing to has 100,000 more followers than me. There's someone else who has 600,000 more followers than her. And, still, there are people who have millions more followers than them both.

It's exhausting, trying to keep up. Trying to find the definition for an indefinable concept. To be "good enough" when good enough is an ever-moving target. To be "good enough" when nobody actually knows what it is to finally be "good enough." To keep running toward an imaginary finish line that disappears into the horizon even when it seems close enough to touch.

And yet, don't we all, online and offline, play this game with ourselves? Try to find the invisible "good enough" point, believing that it exists. What is enough money? Enough followers? Enough achievement? Enough friends? Enough accolades? Enough impressive shit? When does it ever feel like *enough*?

There's a visual that happens in my mind when I get this intense feeling of insecurity. What happens is I feel like all these beautiful parts of me that make me unique get pulled out of me, like multicolored threads, and they go to other people. They scatter. They stop belonging to me. I lose my color; it seems to seep from me. I get an empty feeling. And when I remind myself that I am not going to play at the unwinnable game, I watch as I collect the threads and add them back to me, and I feel full again.

Social media is a perfect microcosm of invisible, unwinnable games. It's the perfect opportunity to completely lose your peace of mind. We all know that social media is a specific kind of detriment to our well-being, mental health, and self-esteem. And that is because it's designed to be unwinnable, just like so many other things that keep us striving, and proving, and trying to collect enough validation to be crowned "good enough."

And yet, I am wildly ambitious. And yet, I do want my words read by lots and lots of people. And yet, genuinely, my artistic work gives me immense joy and pleasure. And yet, I am driven. And yet, there is still so much more I want to give to this world, and to myself.

It can be easy to be this way, and give all my threads away. I so desperately wanted to be good enough for so long, even if the definition was amorphous. I just wanted to feel it. The promised land. Good enough. Finally.

So, how do I reconcile my ambition with all of this? Well, I refuse to be dissatisfied. I work on the balance between my dreams and my present life, which is to say that I don't fuel my dreams with a sort of loathing of my current life. Whenever I start to think, "I'll be good when I get to that place this person on social media is at," I don't let that thought crystallize into a story. I stop it before it becomes an internalized belief.

I don't want to play the game.

No.

I *cannot* and *will not* play the game.

When I have a painful belief, I am tasked to change my mind about the thing that is hurting me. Too often we take our internal stories as irrefutable truth, when they are likely societal conditioning we have yet to interrogate within.

I either need to change my mind and my approach about social media, or I need to leave it altogether. Those are my only two options. At this point, I am unavailable for harming myself, for letting my ambition be bigger than my well-being. There is nothing out there that's going to give me permission to think I am good enough. Thinking that way is harmful. I can no longer live in a mind that is constantly causing me pain.

Therefore, I have to change my mind.

It's as simple, and as difficult, as that.

When I am not caught in the crossfire of an unexpected fire of insecurity, here's how I look at social media now. Here's how I changed my mind, and what I remind myself of when I start trying to win the unwinnable "good enough" game.

I can focus on the "negative" parts of social media, like the comparison, the people trading in envy, the aspirational lives, the highlight reels, the impossible standards. That all exists, on social media and elsewhere. Wherever I go, that will exist. It's up to me to decide whether I'll let it affect me. It's up to me to decide what my reaction to all of that will be. That is my power. And it is yours, too.

Or, I can fix my focus on different parts of social media that are actually infused with joy, learning, and optimism. If I follow the right kind of people for where I'm at, I can see possibilities for my life and mind-set that I would never have seen. Representation is so important, because without it we have a hard time knowing what is possible. At any given moment, I can see women living in a way that is inspiring. Without media gatekeepers, voices that would have otherwise been silenced get to come through on social media. It is a place where I can be inspired, educated, seen, and represented.

I felt like an outsider for a very long time. Like I was too much, too emotional, too sensitive. And yet, social media has shown me that there are so many other people like me, who care, who think deeply, who idealize a better world. This has made me feel so much less isolated. It has made me braver. It has given me a voice that I may not have given myself without it.

Social media can feel like a competition in my unhealed moments.

Or, in my most freed, healed moments, it feels like a beautiful collaboration. A patchwork of art and learning from voices that have been silenced for far too long, from people who have created their own opportunities instead of waiting to be chosen. When you share your art online, you choose yourself. It's unprecedented—the way we can choose ourselves online. The way we can find our people. The way we can be exposed to so many beautiful words and works of art that, just a decade ago, would have had to be chosen by gatekeepers in order for us to see them.

In my most freeing moments, I see myself as adding to the patchwork of collaboration that is social media. I get to connect with people from all over the world. I get to expose my writing to lots and lots of people. I don't need to ask for permission from anyone in order to share my words. I don't need some old white guy at the helm of some magazine or newspaper to tell me that my words matter. I get to decide my value.

I have a career because of the internet. I have a career that, even when I was in college, didn't exist yet.

There are lots of things to dislike about social media. I'm not saying there's nothing that can be changed or improved upon. What I'm saying is that we can change our mind about how we approach virtually everything. We can see the bad outcomes, focus on them, give them more credence and weight. We can believe that the worst of something is the truest of it.

Or we can see the good outcomes, and focus on those.

Almost everything can produce a pro/con list. Nothing is a universal good or bad. It simply comes down to, internally, which column of the list we give more weight to.

Often, we give the most weight to the cons, the negatives, the parts that aren't working, usually to our own emotional detriment. I used to be like that. I had an edge, a pessimism. I thought my sadness was always truer than my happiness. I believed my anger carried more weight than my joy. And I thought that being positive meant being delusional.

I'm not a "good vibes only" person—even now. All vibes are allowed. I can see the negative parts of social media, while at the same time deciding to interact with the positive parts. I can hear my trickier emotions while understanding that I always want to return to calm as a set point. I am in chorus with my emotions, but I only truly identify with the ones that make me feel good. I fuel those more. I give myself more encouragement than I do critique. I let my anger become positive action. I allow my emotions to fuel my next steps. I choose where I put my focus.

I heal my way through the insecurity of this morning. I listen to it. And instead of denying it, or bypassing it, I used it here. It became the fuel for this chapter.

That, to me, feels like peace. It feels like being in the flow of my life, instead of thrashing against the tide of it.

It is within my power to decide where I focus. I might get distracted by something else, or pulled into the emotion, or given the chance to heal, but I decide where I give the most weight. That is my power—and it is yours, too.

You do not need to keep harming yourself. If there is a part of your life (or many parts) that feel like daggers, blunt the edge of them. Change your mind about how you approach it. Change your mind about how much focus you're giving it. Change your mind about how much it matters. How often we give up this power. How often we forget or don't know that we are that powerful, that our minds are *this* fierce.

You could unfollow every single person on your social media channels and refollow only the people who feel the most uplifting and inspiring to you. And you can watch as your entire worldview changes just from the exposure to different viewpoints. Is that not powerful? And yet, we are so used to feeling bad about ourselves, so comfortable with being our own worst enemy, that we don't even take a step forward like this. We follow celebrities and influencers whose lives make us feel inadequate. We think that jealousy makes us motivated. Yet all it's doing is causing a disconnect within.

Refuse to harm yourself. That's the beginning of this kind of change. Make your mind a home that supports you. It's startling that we can change our minds about nearly everything, that we can interpret a situation in whatever way we desire, that we can have vastly different reactions to the same experience. You can change your mind. It's not easy, but it's possible, and entirely worth the effort.

You can choose to think thoughts that affirm you. You can change who you get your inspiration from. You can see your life through a totally different lens. It's all available to you. It's only a disservice to you to pretend as though you don't have this power. Your mind is creating reality. On social media, many different realities are available to consume, interpret, and take inspiration from. Once you start choosing the ones that make you feel good, so much can change.

"Good enough" is too elusive. It's like quicksilver. You grab it, only to find it falls through your fingers. The only real thing to do is stop trying to be "good enough" and make your life so wonderful it's no longer a consideration. Stop giving your power to others, assuming their life is better than yours. How do you know? And what is that "better" definition based on? Interrogate everything. Be vigilant about your thoughts.

What you consume, ends up consuming you.

Make sure you consume all the best words, the best art, the inspiration. Make sure you consume what makes you feel good.

I swear you deserve it.

Change your mind completely. Claim that power. Don't you dare give it up.

CHAPTER 7

Shame Motivates Me

OFTEN, WITHOUT CONSCIOUSLY REALIZING IT, we use shame to motivate ourselves into making changes. We shame ourselves as a form of inspiration to fuel us into becoming who we wish we were or in an effort to prove something. Shame is the "should" voice. I should be further along. I should have a "better" body. I shouldn't take any time off. My life should look like that person's life.

The logic, then, is that if we have these "shoulds," then we will be motivated to do enough to eradicate the should. If we lose weight, the shame about our body will go away. If we get some external achievement, the shame about where we're at in life will go away. If we get this thing, the shame will go away.

Basically: If we can get something out there, the inner turmoil will be reconciled.

And yet, breaking it down this way, we know it's not true.

Shame is extremely sneaky. And it makes sense to think that the shame is popping up in our consciousness in order to motivate us to make a change.

But shame is not motivating. It's a guise and a myth. When you try to prove your own self-hatred or self-loathing wrong, all you do is create a story for yourself that you have to *earn* your self-esteem and worthiness and love. It might help you get to some short-term solutions and results, but ultimately it doesn't change your internal belief. It doesn't rewrite the story you are telling yourself.

Shame as a motivator works. It does. There's a reason so many of us adopt it. We try to do and achieve and "busy" our way out of that creeping, sinking feeling of shame. And for a while, it works. The shame dissipates, but until it's pulled out from the root, until it hits the open air, until it's really heard and felt and faced, it will keep growing and multiplying.

Shame might work for a while, but there's a better way.

Facing the shame and going toward something positive works infinitely better.

As I've written about, I spent a couple decades of my life struggling to accept and love my body. I grew up in the Age of the Pop Star and internalized the beauty standards of the early aughts—taut abs, blonde hair, thin, always thin. When I got into my twenties, there was a whispering of body acceptance, but in no way was it the mainstream conversation it is now. So, I was taught to hate my body. My unruly body. The body that just did not metabolize food the same way as my skinny friends. I would be eating carrot sticks and plain turkey for lunch while my thin best friend downed a Big Mac and then ate a bowl of Frosted Flakes as an after-school snack.

Shame became my home.

I was bullied in elementary and middle school because of my weight. I started my first diet at ten years old. I didn't have a boyfriend in high school, and I remember my mind was filled with insecurity, so much so that I became a poor student, preferring to banish myself to the shadows than be seen in the body I was told was wrong. I just remember all of high school being loud for me—a loud chorus of self-hatred, like I'd finally been broken down long enough that I believed everyone. I was not attractive. I was not good enough. My body would never be loved. I would never be loved.

The summer before I went to college, I worked out for four hours per day, every single day. I obsessively tracked every morsel of food that I ate. It wasn't my first diet, and it wouldn't be my last, but I was motivated. Everyone was so proud of me. I was losing weight, my body was changing, and I went to college twenty pounds lighter than when I graduated from high school.

This was going to be my reinvention.

The first thing I did on the first weekend was get drunk and make out with the first guy who seemed interested. I was 180 pounds then. I remember that number, because that number for years to come would haunt me.

In college, I became a new woman. The weight loss had spurred something on within me, a sort of determination to not be who I had been in my hometown. I wanted to be fun and carefree and attractive and desirable. I wanted to be the girl that I'd seen my friends be, that I felt I could never be, that I felt my body had prevented me from being.

I lost myself a thousand different ways that first year of college, overcompensating for all the experiences I felt I had missed out on in high school. I partied, I drank, I hooked up. I was *wanted*. The noise in my mind that had been with me all through my childhood—that thrumming of insecurity I carried in my body— quieted down long enough for me to somewhat and hazily experience life.

I went to this one party early on at the start of the fall semester and I remember everyone talking, laughing, drinking, and enjoying the atmosphere. I sat on the couch staring at a plate of chocolate chip cookies, willing myself not to eat one. I was not kind to myself about the way I wanted a cookie. I told myself I was disgusting, that I shouldn't eat like this, that I'd lose everything, that I wasn't good enough, that I didn't deserve that cookie yet. The party merrily carried along and I was in my own world, me against this plate of cookies. I was mesmerized by the shame of it, the hunger within me, the dichotomy of wanting to be free and yet knowing my freedom meant a body that the world hated.

I remember being perversely happy with myself that I didn't succumb to temptation and eat a cookie that night. My own shame had worked. I shamed myself into not eating that cookie.

But then, I started to enjoy college. I got busy. I got a job, I went to class, I made friends. And I let loose a little. I stopped going to the gym as much. I wasn't as vigilant about what I was eating. Soon, the weight I'd lost over the summer started to creep back on. I stopped weighing myself. And I silenced the shame that started to become a deafening roar with alcohol, and busyness, and the pursuit of hookups.

I gained more weight, and so began a toxic cycle of shame that took over a decade to break.

Here's how it would go: I hate my body and feel shame > I know I need to change my body > I take an action to change my body because I'm trying to get away from the shame > The shame goes away temporarily, and I stop doing whatever I started > I hate my body and feel shame.

I did the same thing with my writing. I'd feel shame that I wasn't writing more, so I'd sit down and force myself to write for a few days in a row. The shame would subside, and then I'd stop again. And it would repeat. This cycle became addictive, and the only one I knew. This cycle that I had subconsciously convinced myself was "working" became the cycle I used to do anything and everything I thought I "should" be doing.

Shame was my motivation.

It became my *sole* motivation.

And then it became something I relied on, thinking that if I eliminated my shame then I'd become complacent and lazy.

Years later, when I confronted myself with the proposition to be happy above all else, I knew that the shame cycle had to go. I wasn't keeping promises to myself at all. I wasn't doing things for my well-being. I was only taking actions that were appeasing this vast well of shame within me.

I wasn't going toward anything good; I was simply outrunning the shame.

I suspect that a lot of us do this, but it's ingrained and subconscious. It's not something we interrogate, because it does, in many ways, *work*. A lot of us can spend a lot of time and a lot of effort outrunning shame. It can feel incredibly motivating. It's so enticing to prove our past rejections wrong. To try to earn our way out of a feeling of unworthiness. The formula seems so simple: If I can just get there, then I won't feel bad about myself anymore.

But, shame cannot be healed by an outrunning. It can't be proven wrong. It has to be faced, looked at, and processed. Avoidance only strengthens it.

Shame is a feeling that is not easy to target and identify. It's a sort of shrinking in the body. It's not a feeling a lot of us want to readily claim. It is, by nature, a bad feeling. We feel shame for feeling shame. The circuitry breeds and multiplies it.

When I decided to feel good and stop the shame cycle, I had nothing left that I could prove or earn. My shame cycle stopped when I brought the shame into the light. When I faced that shame. What power was I giving my body? What stories about my body was I taking on? Where does this shame come from, and where did I pick it up? Who told me my body was "bad" and "wrong"? And is it not my responsibility to now change my relationship with my body? I can't control what happened to me when I was younger, but I can control how I relate to myself now. I can control how I view my body now. And I refused to keep feeling ashamed for my body. It wasn't getting me anywhere. It wasn't contributing to a solution. It wasn't even motivating me to do much of anything. I was cloaked in shame, struggling against the quicksand of it.

I stopped believing what the world had told me about my body. And I started to live within my own truth.

I did this with so many other aspects of my life I wanted to change. Like getting out of debt and creating financial freedom. Like actually writing with discipline. Shame does not motivate me to make any changes now. I make changes in my life because I love myself, not because I am ashamed of myself and think if I change something external that shame will go away. My own love works better.

I had to find new ways to motivate myself. The "I won't feel like shit anymore" mantra of before wasn't going to work. I had unveiled shame and it no longer held as much appeal for me.

Shame does that—it expands the fear and makes you lose touch with reality.

Shame can be disorienting. It can distort everything.

But, facing the shame is *freeing*. Shame does not like truth.

If you think shame is motivating, truth is going to blow your mind.

I had to go toward the good things, the true things. I focused on the freedom of being at peace in my body. The freedom of being out of debt. The feel of stacking up pages of writing.

I went in pursuit of *wonderful* things.

And it taught me a valuable lesson about motivation.

I exercised in mild, unpredictable spurts when shame motivated me.

I got snippets of writing onto the computer when I was outrunning shame.

I paid down one credit card in ten years by using shame as a motivator.

But when I started going toward the good things, when I started pulling up the roots of my shame, *that's* when my life exploded in surprising and beautiful ways.

I started exercising regularly for my well-being, as opposed to punishing myself for feeling shame (or punishing my body for not being thin). In the past, I had always started a new exercise regime based on what would make me feel less shame, and what would help me lose weight faster. When I stopped feeling shame around my body, I realized that I am actually athletic and love to be active. I had missed out on years of being active because shame had robbed me of it. Because shame had told me I should only do exercise I hate in order to have a thin body I can finally love. I never enjoyed exercise because I was always doing the exercise in order to outrun the shame. I never got any of the positive benefits from it, like the improved mental outlook or energetic boost. I was just exercising with resentment, trying to get away from that feeling of shame.

Now, four years later, being active and exercising regularly is one of the best things I do for my mental, emotional, and physical well-being. Shame may have given me a few weeks a year of exercise, but pulling out the root of shame gave me years of consistency.

I assumed that letting go of the shame cycle would make me lazy and complacent. A lot of us think this without perhaps knowing we even do. It's an insidious belief created under the guise of motivation. We think that the one thing keeping us going is the past version of us we're trying to outrun. If only we could prove that one person wrong. If only we could prove to our parents we're worthy. If only we could rewrite the past with our current successes.

It doesn't really work that way. Trying to get to a place where you don't feel shame without *looking* at the shame is like chasing after a carrot on a fishing pole. There's always someone yanking that pole back further and further. It's meant to be impossible.

Shame does not like truth. It does not like to be revealed. Shame breeds in the shadows. A lot of us believe admitting to the shame makes us weak. That doing so might make us lose our edge. We think the shame is what is keeping it all together.

But actually, the strongest thing you can possibly do is stay in the present moment, stop trying to earn your way out of shame, and simply sit with it. Bring it out into the open air. Let it hit the light. Examine it and see the root of it. Who told you this? Who made you feel this? Who convinced you of this shame? Why is it there? And what do you think it's serving?

It won't be easy. But it's a lot harder to live your life outrunning shame. Because not only does it never work, it's also exhausting. It'll wear you down.

So, lay that expectation down. Know that on the other side of shame is a surprising freedom—and all the things that feel like a chore right now, that feel impossible, that plague you, will become so much easier to tackle once you can remove the shame around them.

Releasing yourself from the shame of being human and making mistakes gives you your whole humanity back.

Everything you thought you wanted to do in service of outrunning shame becomes a lot lighter. Bringing shame out into the light is clarifying. It's purifying. And your life and soul will be better for it once you do.

CHAPTER 8

Self-love Is Pretty, and Easy

I'VE LEARNED THAT OUTRUNNING, or trying to disprove, self-hatred will not be the basis of a happy life. We cannot do enough external things in order to love ourselves. It has to come from within. Which means motivation for any change has to come from a place of love.

In the past, when I've hated myself, I thought I could do enough out there in the world to love myself, that I could earn my own love. I now know how fruitless that pursuit is. And how it simply doesn't work. I have to love myself exactly as I am, exactly where I am.

But this idea of self-love is something we're sold all the time. Lose weight, and then you get to love your body. Get the dream job, and then you get to love your life. Or just try to collect enough approval from other people so that you feel like your life has meaning and value.

The "self" part of self-love is the important part. It's an inside job. People say that, and it's true, but what does it really mean?

It means that all the time we spend trying to earn our love out there, in the world, is not ever going to accumulate so that we can finally look at ourselves and say, "You know what? Enough people like me, I think I can like me now, too." This moment does not happen. If it did, don't you think it would have happened already? Maybe you know what it feels like to have someone else's adoration and not be able to access it for yourself. To not be able to feel as loved as you logically know that you are. It's beautiful to be loved by others, but it's hard to accept that love when we don't love ourselves. It's hard trying to get enough of other people's love in order to confirm something we don't feel within. It's hard trying to change ourselves constantly, try to find the magic pill, try to become enough, be enough, do enough—in order to finally have our own love click in.

It's so hard.

And yet so many of us spend years—decades, lifetimes—trying to do just that.

Which means that whatever you're trying to get out there is something you can access within. And that might be a frustrating truth to have to come to—but, inevitably, it's the most freeing detail. It's the freedom in which you can build all the most beautiful things in your life. Because when you are loved and you already love yourself, you can feel the love. When good things happen to you, you can feel them. You don't have to worry about deserving them. You love you and that is your foundation. That is your freedom.

When you love you, all the good in your life becomes amplified. Self-love is so much less about face masks and bubble baths and so much more about the unlearning. Self-love is our natural state.

It's just that we've been born into a world that convinces us to hate ourselves.

It's just that we've been taught to abandon ourselves.

It's just that we've forgotten that loving ourselves works better.

Self-love brings more joy. More fulfillment. More of everything.

When I met Houssem, I was on a low-carb diet with a nutritionist and had lost forty pounds. It was 2011, in Paris, France, and I was twenty-five years old. Houssem came into my life like a whirlwind, energy and confidence and immersive love, right from the beginning. It was terrifying and electric. He didn't speak English, but this went beyond words. We didn't need words. We felt our way into falling in love, which could have been a terrible idea, if our love weren't still enduring, ten-plus years later.

Every morning, Houssem liked to eat a plate of scrambled eggs, yogurt that he'd shake before eating, apple juice, and a fresh baguette from any one of the local boulangeries that were near us in Paris. I hadn't eaten much bread in a long time. Months. I had convinced myself that string cheese was better than bread. That I could live off cold cuts and cucumbers.

But then I sank my teeth into a fresh baguette and something fell away. A determination. The hard edge I'd developed in my quest for thinness. That one bite of baguette turned into many bites. Turned into croissants. Turned into kebab sandwiches with samurai sauce and fries dipped in mayo. I let loose my hunger as I let myself fall in love with this mysterious and alluring man who came from a country I couldn't yet find on the map. He spoke fast Arabic and was always on the phone with a cousin or his mom or his sister or a friend. He laughed with abandon on the phone. I longed to understand him, to know what made him laugh like that, to be loved by someone so obviously loved by others.

It was not easy for me to be loved, though. I wasn't in the "right" body yet. I still had more weight to lose. I wasn't "supposed" to be loved like this. Not in a body that couldn't fit into any of the clothes in the Parisian shops.

And yet we'd walk along the streets of Paris and he'd sling his long arm around mine, making me feel seen and held in a way I never had before. He'd kiss me while we rode up the escalator. He'd stroke my cheek with the side of his hand. He'd tap his chest to have me come lie there in the evenings. He was so expressive, so intimate, so affectionate. I didn't know how to process it. I didn't think I was supposed to have my body loved in this way. He wasn't overly attached to my body. It wasn't like a fetish. He just saw me. And from the moment we met, he did not let go.

I didn't yet have the kind of self-esteem to really understand this affectionate, overt display of love.

Subconsciously, I was filling up a hole. As a teenager, I'd grown to hate myself and blamed my lack of a love life on being unattractive. I had then assumed that if I could get enough attention from men (and some women) that I'd finally prove it wrong. I thought that if enough people wanted to sleep with me or desire me or want me or date me, then . . . I'd love myself.

I tried to collect the attention. I'd recite it back to myself at night when I would try to fall asleep and my heart would race from the anxiety I was actively ignoring. I'd think of stolen kisses on drunken nights and I'd remember words whispered into my ear from lovelorn men and I'd remember the women I never expected to be curious to always want their curiosity fulfilled by me and I'd fill myself up on their validation.

I'd try to hold on to it, hoping it might stick.

Look at all the proof. Look at how desired I am. Look at all these people who want and wanted me. Am I allowed to love myself yet?

And then it became, *well, maybe I want something real.* Maybe if someone loves me, like *really* loves me, I'll love me. The week before I met Houssem I had developed a terrible cold. I was lonelier than I could ever remember. I wished I had someone, anyone, to care for me. I'd been alone for so long, carrying it around like a badge of honor. Like if they don't want to love me, I don't want their love.

The very day I felt better, I met this amazing man who held me so gently and tenderly that my heart sort of broke every time he did it. It hurt for him to love me. It hurt nearly every day. Because I didn't love me. So I couldn't reconcile any of it. Why did he love me? He had no words to tell me without a common language. He couldn't do anything but show me, and I couldn't believe any of it. Even if he had the words, my mind would have twisted them.

I almost wanted him to leave me, just so I wouldn't have to reconcile the feeling within me that was so deeply disconnected from the love I was receiving. You don't have to love yourself before you love someone else, but let me tell you, it helps if you do.

It's unbelievably difficult to accept the kind of love you don't think you deserve.

And I had been wrong. There weren't enough men and women in the world to convince me I was worth loving. I had tried it. I had worked hard to get all sorts of attention and none of it did the deep work.

I had searched for my worth in all sorts of places, but none more fervently than in the approval from men.

The formula was this: As a woman, my entire value hinges on

my body and my looks. My body would not become what I wanted it to become even when I starved it. So, if I could get enough men to want me, then I could prove my body was neither a problem nor a hindrance. Therefore, my body would have value. Therefore, I'd have value. Therefore, I'd be worthy.

But not even Houssem could convince me. All he did was shine a floodlight on where I was not in possession of myself.

So, I ate.

Maybe it was for comfort. Maybe it was for control. Maybe it was to test whether Houssem would still love me if I gained back the weight I'd lost. I don't really know. All I know is that for the next ten years I'd be within the grasp of a very sneaky, almost imperceptible binge-eating disorder that I kept returning to for punishment, for comfort, for control.

There had been many reasons I had been taught to hate myself. I had internalized some, tried to prove some wrong, and ultimately the disassociation, the distractions, the escapism, and the avoidance all stemmed from my inability to process the many ways a woman must behave, must show up, and must conform.

Many times, I had buckled under the weight of all those expectations, all the many contradictions. Like with my body—it was "unacceptable" to be a woman in a larger body. We were scorned and the butt of jokes on TV shows and in movies. But to be a woman who was conventionally beautiful (and thin, always thin) seemed harsh as well. The need to keep it up. The value on just the body. The ever-changing standards of how the body must curve; where it should be flat and where it should jut out.

It seemed impossible to keep up with any of it, trying to contort into an ideal and make sure to stay there, to have a whole life and livelihood built upon the ability to shave the body down to something the world deemed "good enough." And then, once you got there, that same body became a commodity, an object, something for others to claim and monetize and exploit.

There just never seemed to be viable options. And that was just with my body. Careers were a whole other mountain to climb as a woman. Who we got to be and who we disappointed by our choices. Navigating the world as a woman, being scared to walk alone, feeling watched, feeling desperate to be visible and also terrified to be so. Then, babies, and marriage, and families, and the many ways we can disappoint others with our choices there. Was it feminist to stay at home with kids? Was it feminist to forgo a family for career? Was it feminist to be expected to do it all, with a smile on our face?

I felt like the "wrong" kind of woman. That other women knew how to "women" better than me. They knew how to curl their hair, wear high heels, brutalize their body into submission, and somehow navigate this impossible world with all its many changing definitions and pressures.

I thought it was essential to be a woman who hated herself. Like anything else would be selfish. Like anything else would be impossible.

That's how ingrained it was.

Over the years, I learned to love myself in pieces. I tolerated my body, from certain angles, and in some situations. I took control of my finances. I learned that real self-care wasn't baths and face masks, but was the boring, unsexy things like doing your taxes and paying your bills and making to-do lists you can actually complete. I started listening to myself and to my emotions as best I could. I exercised consistently as a way to feel good and divested myself (constantly, relentlessly) of the obsession with weight loss. I learned to say nice things to myself. I learned to keep my own promises. I learned to be my own friend, to support myself, to celebrate my forward momentum, even if it was slow and small and not shiny at all to other people. I learned to take pictures of myself, to like them, to not stare at them for hours and notice every flaw and feel that shrinking sense of loathing.

I learned that self-love is a lot more torrential than I expected. It's an unpeeling, an unlearning, a healing process that means you have to come face to face with all the reasons you don't feel worthy of your own love, in order to process and heal them. Self-love wasn't as pretty as it sounded. It was painful. It was a tearing from an identity, from a status quo, from the breathless need I had to be "normal" and "acceptable."

I had spent decades avoiding that exact reckoning.

To walk directly into the fire—it was terrible before it was freeing.

And yet, through all this progress and healing, my relationship with my body still existed in some other place. I was me, Jamie, and then I had this body, which felt foreign and strange. I wasn't connected to it. I wasn't doing what was best for my physical health. I was neglecting my body, but my version of self-love hadn't reached my body yet. It was a wound that felt too tender to touch and explore.

And then the pandemic of 2020 happened, and everything in lockdown got to be too much and suddenly my only joy was food. Food dulled everything. Food made everything blunt and easy to digest and it was a place to escape to.

When we had moved back to Los Angeles from France in 2019, within a few months I found a therapist I could see bimonthly.

During 2020, I was "seeing" my therapist by phone every other week. I missed the in-person sessions, but I was glad to have already been in therapy by the time the pandemic and lockdown hit Los Angeles.

It was September 2020 and the summer had been a brutal and relentless onslaught of horrifying news. The external world reflected my internal world. I was at war with myself, and the external world only amplified it. Houssem left for a weekend to visit a friend in San Francisco and I turned into a different person. I had been eating quite a bit during the pandemic, vaguely aware that food had once again become a crutch that I could not control, but I wasn't ready to confront that yet. Every time my mind wanted to notice it, I'd disassociate from myself with more food, more TV.

That weekend, I ate a lot. And the same way an alcoholic might hit rock bottom, I felt a shift within me. This was harming me. This was unkind. This was not loving. This was not "self-care." This was not who I wanted to continue to be. I felt sick. I felt ashamed. And I felt that the only thing I could do was let this experience hit the open air.

I had to tell my therapist.

I was shaking. I felt the shame move its way through my body in waves. I spoke it out loud. The eating. The feeling that food was my only joy. The way I used food to take all the noise within myself and out in the world and dull it into something manageable. The way it didn't feel like it was "working" as well as it used to. That it no longer felt like a viable defense mechanism.

I told her all of that.

I said, "I think I have a binge-eating disorder."

She agreed that I might. And she didn't hang up the phone in disgust, didn't tsk me, didn't gasp at me. I'd let the most honest and shameful thing about me hit the open air—and absolutely nothing terrible happened.

Except I felt lighter.

I felt relieved to have said it out loud.

I felt I could finally admit that the way I was treating my body was not the way I wanted to keep treating my body. I didn't harangue my past self. I forgave her. She did the best she could with the knowledge she had. She tried. And for years she had done the thing that she felt was best: She worked on her relationship with her body from the inside out. Now, it was time to take care of my physical body, not just my emotional one.

That's the other thing about self-love—it's not a fixed position. It's not static. You grow, you become, you change, you unpeel a layer to find another layer, and you keep unpeeling, becoming and unbecoming. We are not meant to stay one way forever. What can feel like neglect one year feels like safety in another. What can feel like comfort in one season of life can feel like constriction in another.

What for years had felt like a loving relationship with my body stopped feeling loving in that moment in time. I had to revise my relationship with food. I had to find a new way to interact with the scale, with clothing sizes, with exercise. I'd unpeeled a lot of layers, but that one had been at the core of something. My relationship with food had been something deep, something enduring, something I'd grabbed at to deal with being sexually assaulted at a young age, the demands of the world, shame, fear, all of it—and it stopped being effective.

That's something my therapist told me that helped: This had been an effective way to deal with life for me. The food had been a comfort—and that's okay. It's okay to not be ready for the big healing yet. We need to leave space for that to be true as well.

Letting that truth air out, it felt like a completion of a cycle of almost ten years. I remembered Paris and meeting Houssem and that first torn piece of a baguette that he handed me while we walked on the cobblestoned streets a block from my little basement studio. I remember escaping to food to handle the pressure of trying to be loved. I remember how it helped me dull out and quiet and abandon the part of myself that wouldn't let this steady, gentle man love me.

Speaking with my therapist, and then continuing on the deep healing around food, I began to unlock that part of myself. I began to let that part be loved, too. I reconnected with pieces of myself that I'd abandoned along the way. And I loved even those parts.

Self-love asks us to unveil the shadows within us. It asks us to bring it all out into the light and determine how we feel about it now. It asks us to redefine who we are to ourselves.

And in being truthful, in being open and receptive, we can learn to love all the parts of ourselves that we were taught to abandon and dislike and separate from out of shame. Self-love, then, in many ways, is an integration of all the pieces of us.

Self-love is refusing to harm myself any longer. Recognizing that I have learned systems of harm, and I don't have to keep perpetuating it for myself.

The conclusions that you have come to are not the conclusions you need to keep coming to. Think about that. Think about how you are forming patterns. Think about what you take as some sort of ultimate truth. "I'm just not ready for that." "I'm such a mess." "I'm always anxious." "Things don't work out for me." Even if you have evidence to support these statements, you likely have evidence to support the opposite, too. So why not focus on the flip side? We lose our power when we deny ourselves that choice.

But that's how we survive, especially us women—we break ourselves up into digestible pieces, leaving parts that we don't think will be accepted and liked to fend for themselves. We can feel so fragmented, so disconnected from the whole of ourselves. Maybe that's the crisis point. The recognition that we are fragmented, and that we discarded the pieces that other people deemed unworthy and unacceptable.

Self-love, then, is a putting back together. An alignment. A discard of the expectations other people gave us that we no longer want to carry. And a reunion with the parts of us we deserted that we do want to carry now. That we want to rehabilitate now. That we want to love now.

Self-love is wholeness.

It's healing toward that wholeness.

And not letting your truth live in the shadows any longer.

CHAPTER 9

I Should Feel Guilty

UNCONSCIOUSLY, WE HAVE A TENDENCY to take on a lot of guilt. Guilt is the course correction for the people pleaser. Something I have has triggered an unsavory feeling in you? Okay, let me shrink a bit. And women, in particular, take on guilt in order to appease others. It's so subtle, the way we guilt ourselves out of the things we enjoy and desire.

The language of guilt is: "Why me?"

The language of deserving is: "Why *not* me?"

There's a lot of inner truth you'll ignore when it comes at the price of guilt. When that inner truth makes you feel bad. When you may have to step into the type of person that is going to do what is best for you regardless of how that is interpreted by others. Caring about your own life is not selfish. And yet, many people have been guilted into believing that if they put their own needs ahead of others, then it's a selfish thing. And they "should" (shame language) feel guilty about doing so. Guilt evens it out. Guilt keeps you small and contained. Guilt will keep you in your "place."

Especially when it's the type of inner truth that will have consequences for other people in your life, the type of people that have benefited from you not having boundaries, or needs, or opinions on how you'd like to be treated. When it's the type of people that like you a little miserable, a little unexpressed, a little smaller than them.

When it's the type of inner truth that's asking you to rise, and ascend, and let go of the crushing need to have everyone like and accept you.

When it's the type of inner truth that might upset people.

When it's you choosing yourself over the needs of everyone else.

Guilt will try to course-correct you back to pleasing others. Don't let it. You are not required to feel guilty for caring about your own life. You deserve that. You are not a martyr to everyone else's needs. Yes, it's great to nourish and care for others, but not to the detriment of your own nourishment and care. You do not need to sacrifice yourself at the altar of everyone else's expectations of you.

I grew up Catholic, so guilt has lived in my bones for most of my life. Guilt about what I'd eaten. Guilt about my cravings—carnal and otherwise. Guilt about what I was or was not doing. The guilt was like a labyrinth, and I'd get lost in it, unable to find the exit. It was just a heavy burden, a weighted blanket, that was foisted upon my shoulders unwittingly.

My guilt was always external. What will other people think? Of me? Of how I'm acting? How I'm eating? Will they think I'm selfish? It was a sort of constant monitoring of my own image in other people's eyes. And also, a way of keeping myself a little more contained so that nobody ever got jealous of me, or thought I'd become "too good" for them.

How I longed to outgrow people, and past versions of myself— and how terrified I was to do so.

Because I experienced so many painful rejections in my past, my empathic little heart couldn't handle the idea of me doing *anything* that would hurt someone else, even if I did so without knowing or without meaning to. That fear became guilt, which became a way of grounding me, of bringing me back to where I "belong" and not letting me ever get too far away from that scared girl who just wanted to be liked.

If I could make everyone else happy, maybe they'd never experience what I did. And if I could keep the guilt mechanism humming, then I would be safe. I wouldn't have to rise up to my potential, or stand out, or use all my gifts and talents to their fullest expression. I'd shine a little less, if that meant I could make someone else feel better. I'd stay in the mire of misery so that I could be relatable. I'd befriend anyone and everyone even if they didn't make me feel good, simply because I never wanted to cause anyone any kind of pain. Or hurt anyone. Or reject anyone.

Which meant I absorbed all the pain, hurt, and rejection I was deflecting from them.

I was in pain from living cramped.

I was hurt by my own denial.

And I rejected *myself* in order to be accepted by *them*. Whoever "them" was at the time. It always changed. It always seemed to morph.

Don't worry, even if you think I'm doing well, I'm in pain from this and this and this. Don't worry, in that moment of celebration, I also felt crushing self-doubt. Don't worry, you may see my writing going viral on the internet, but I'm getting paid abysmally. Don't worry. Don't worry. Don't worry—my life isn't really *that* good.

And so I made it true. I tainted every good moment with the guilt layer. It became normal, a thing I did involuntarily. Every compliment was deflected into a complaint. And I made sure that absolutely no one thought I was *enjoying* any of the success I was experiencing, *especially* me.

I became so good at this I didn't even realize I was doing it.

I had been martyring myself without awareness.

At the very core of my inability to truly embody my happiness was this ever-present, ever-vibrating guilt.

That it was not safe to do well. That actually it was selfish to care much about my own happiness. That actually I'm supposed to serve others.

Other people did not want to see me do well. Other people would not like me if I did well. Other people would reject me if I liked myself too much. Other people don't like women when they are happy, when they know their value, when they derive worth from inside of themselves, instead of waiting to be chosen.

Therefore, I had concluded: It's not safe to be happy.

Because I wanted to be liked and accepted more than I wanted nearly anything else.

A memory came to the surface for me in this time of discovery. I was in my junior year of college. There was this advertising competition team that I had joined my freshman year. Typically, it was a year-long extracurricular that only graduating seniors could be a part of, but when I was in my first year I worked in the College of Business and charmed my way into being on the team. By my third year, I'd finally been given the president role.

Essentially, I was the CEO and president of a mock advertising agency. Each year, colleges around the country would compete to put together an advertising and marketing plan for whichever company sponsored the competition. My first year it was Yahoo!. The second year it was Postal Vault. But when I was president, the company was Coca-Cola. Coca-Cola! I was ecstatic. It was my time to put to use everything I had been learning, and I took that seriously.

I gave my classmates homework to complete. I led lectures, the faculty advisor seated in front of me, cramped into a small desk. I wanted to win. California State University, Chico had never won before. When I joined the team, we placed last in the district. We were second place when I was vice president during the Postal Vault year. I wanted to win so badly it became an obsession. This was a three-credit class that lasted two semesters, and yet I gave it all of my time and attention. I believed I *was* the CEO.

The way the class worked was that you get a mock budget from Coca-Cola to use in a multimedia campaign. You had to come up with concepts, marketing figures, and a budget, and put together a multipage plan book with full-color renderings and in-depth explanations of your marketing ideas. It was a complex operation. I had to work with the business and marketing students as well as the communication design ones. Everyone had opinions. And I was detailed, with lofty standards for everyone who was on the team.

I felt that I was shining, but the business students started to pull away. While the business student class was evenly split in terms of gender, the strongest personalities were men, including the faculty advisor who set the tone. I could sense their frustration at me when I was up at the helm of the class, trying to get their attention. The faculty advisor started to make snide comments, disrupting the room even when I was speaking, like I was the teacher and he was the student. I'd prepare presentations on PowerPoint and send out homework that truly needed to get done—and the business students wouldn't do it. I can imagine they probably had lengthy conversations about me after class.

But my desire to win outweighed my desire to be liked. For the first time in my life, the purpose felt greater than these people's approval.

The communication design students liked and respected me. There was always a difference between the creatives and the business students. The former just wanted to make cool designs and the latter—it was all about ego. Thankfully, once the business and marketing students came up with the plan, I spent most of my time with the designers, giving feedback and putting together the plan book.

In late spring, we would give a presentation to a group of judges for the district competition. If we won first place, we'd proceed to the national competition in Louisville, Kentucky. It was too sweet to even think about. We still had to finish the plan book, write and memorize the presentation, and then give it.

I was one of five presenters, which included four other people who took the credit for my work while pretending to be part of a team. They were cold to me on the drive to districts. I sat up front with my advisor, who seemed to dislike me, too.

We gave our presentation. It went flawlessly. I was nervous, but I was on fire. I could feel it buzzing through me—that greatness. I was completely in my element.

The judges deliberated. We won first place. And, unbelievably, out of all the presenters, I won Best Presenter of the entire competition. It was a moment of pure glory for me. It was like my version of winning the Super Bowl and then being named MVP. I was ecstatic.

There was a Q&A with the judges after they announced the standings. It was a teaching moment for all the teams. Some of the other teams asked for feedback on their presentation and plans. I raised my hand and asked the judges, "Do you have any advice for us when we go to nationals?"

The entire room fell silent.

My teammates looked at me with horror.

I think I may have heard a cough across the auditorium—it was breathlessly quiet.

I had no idea what I said was so wrong. We had *won*. We needed advice on how to win at nationals. I thought I was doing us a favor.

I sat up front on the drive back, my teammates in the seats behind me seething with anger. I was wounded by it. I held my Best Presenter plaque against my chest as if it were a shield. All the excitement of that moment of winning, of being the president of a winning team, of being honored for my presentation skills—it all evaporated.

We had a big blowout fight the next time we were all together. They called me a bad leader and a terrible sport, and told me how horrible I was to rub our win in the faces of all the losing teams like that. I felt a wash of shame. Like I had done something unforgivable.

And that experience became a story I carried with me for over a decade.

Winning is unsafe.

And if you win, knowing that you won, being proud of that win, is even more unsafe.

If you win, pretend that you haven't. Be *ashamed* of winning.

No one likes an arrogant woman.

No one likes a woman who knows she has something of worth to offer this world.

No one likes a woman who knows her talent—and how to use it.

No one likes a woman who shines.

I used to cringe thinking about that question I asked, and the silence of that auditorium. It haunted me for years. I'd shrivel just to think about it.

But I realize now that all the shame of that silent room is gone. Instead, I only feel sad that nobody had pulled me aside and told me not to let that moment dim me. I feel sad that I interpreted their anger as anything but abject jealousy. I feel sad that I created a story around what felt possible for me, that I actually believed from that moment on people either liked me or I got to fully express my gifts—I wouldn't be able to have both.

What happened from then is I started to hunch a little more year after year. I did well, but never too well. I kept myself in check. And in that space where my talent wanted to thrive, I felt intense resentment and jealousy for any woman who was able to excel unapologetically. Who did she think she was—just being talented and letting the world see it?

That guilt and shame kept me from unabashedly expressing myself in all the ways I desired, which made me think that I was wasting my potential. I'd think about that competition for years—I was so *promising*. The faculty at the College of Business congratulated me until I graduated. They pulled me aside to talk about my future. But for some, including my own faculty advisor and teammates, it seemed as though my potential was so potent it made grown men feel inferior. That did not feel like a compliment. Now I see it as what it should have been back then to me: fuel.

That story came screeching to the surface as one that had been limiting my happiness and potential for a very long time. The fear of appearing selfish for wanting to win, for wanting to do well, for wanting my gifts acknowledged. Airing it out to myself, letting it hang there, I recognized it for what it was: a group of people who were deeply jealous of me, who made sure I knew that my excellence was dangerous. I don't say that lightly. I don't really like when people are jealous of me, but it's clear in retrospect that I was in my element, and a lot of the men who were in the class did not like to be taking notes from a woman.

The good thing about life is that, while you can't redo your past, you can learn from it, and process it with a new perspective. I will never be able to go back to that silent, tense van ride back to Chico, but I can choose a new way of being when a similar situation comes up. I can start acknowledging my gifts, talents, and abilities and no longer keep them locked away. I can start disappointing people, or upsetting them, just by being me. And I can and have reclaimed what selfish means to me.

I am self-serving, in that I wholeheartedly believe my life is *for* me. And if others don't like me when I do well, it's not on me to change and shift and bend and cramp. It's on me to not care. If people think that those who care about their own happiness are selfish, it's not on me to course-correct with guilt. It's on me to simply keep doing me—and resist the urge to apologize. What do I have to apologize for? That's the world telling me I need to always cramp a little. That's the world shaming me for not being a martyr to the needs of others. It's not on me to live within their ridiculous rules. If caring about my own joy and happiness and healing and fulfillment is selfish, then so be it. I claim that.

Working through this guilt has become a priority for me. I let go of friendships that felt competitive, that benefited from me being a little smaller, a little dimmed out, a little down on my luck. I let go of identities I'd been holding on to—that I was some underdog, that I had to make myself miserable while going after my dreams in order to make sure that my guilt was assuaged. I had to let go of being the martyr, trying to control everyone's feelings by controlling myself. I had to stop rejecting myself. And I had to stop feeling ashamed for being good at things, for having natural abilities, for wanting to shine.

I didn't step out of this guilt overnight. It was a long unbecoming and unlearning. It took multiple years. And that guilt didn't start with the advertising team. They only reinforced it. And it was reinforced hundreds more times in the media—that it is not safe to know your worth as a woman.

It's one thing to have empathy. I have a lot of that. Too much, maybe. I even have a hard time watching soccer games with my husband because I feel bad for the team that loses, every single time. It feels like a curse sometimes.

But empathy can slide itself right into martyrdom if you're not careful. You can be sensitive to other people's experiences, but that doesn't mean you have to lessen your own, or curb your joy, or complain out of habit, or make your happiness seem less than it is.

It's not selfish to do this. I thought it was for a long time.

I remember when Mindy Kaling started *The Mindy Project*. She had created an entire vehicle for herself. She didn't apologize for it. She never deflected. The show felt like a celebration of Mindy owning her genius. As I watched it, I loved it, and also felt this pang of: *Who does Mindy think she is?* She was so confident in that show. Why shouldn't she be?

That show triggered me. I was in awe of it, of her, and also a little angry about it, too. I thought I was just jealous, but it was more than that. I was seeing a woman live in the guilt-free, unapologetic celebration of her genius and talent—and I wanted that.

Kaling looked not only in her element, but also happy to be there. She was not a woman in the business of denying herself the joy of her own gifts. It took me many more years to fully understand my reaction to her and that show. And a few more before I actually stepped into my genius in full.

I started to not only recognize my talent, but learn to enjoy it, too. My talents and gifts and genius were meant for me, too. To enjoy. To express. To celebrate. To love. To benefit me. Without guilt. Or apology.

This isn't selfish. It's *my* life. Your life is allowed to benefit you directly. In fact, it *must*.

You are not here to be a martyr, sacrificing all of your time and energy to make other people's lives more comfortable, bending and breaking in order to do so. You are more than allowed to enjoy your life and admire your talent. You don't have to steep it in self-doubt, make yourself more relatable, tear yourself down so that someone else can feel more comfortable.

See your own potential. Do not wait for someone to give you permission to use your gifts. Step into whatever greatness lives within you, whether it be on a large stage or within the smaller, quieter moments of a beautiful life. Your life is for you. Yes, we can be nurturing to others, and care for them, and be in relationship with lots of people. But, we do not have to be selfless, sacrificial martyrs.

Our lives do not have to be walking apologies.

We are allowed to exist. Exactly as we are. And grow and evolve. And recognize our talents and appreciate them without waiting to be appreciated by others.

That's not selfish.

It's vital.

It's how to stop just surviving—and start really thriving.

PART 2

To Learn....

IN A DISSATISFIED WORLD, unlearning the ways of that world will have a ripple effect that cannot be predicted. My hope is that you marinate on the unlearning part of this book and then use the second part—the learning part—to implement concepts that can provide positive transformations. Unlearning is a process in itself. A necessary and vital one. There's a reason it's the bulk of this book. I never wanted to write a book that didn't get into the mind-set shifts required to be happy in a loud, overwhelming world.

With this next part of the book, I share some of the most powerful, practical shifts you can make in your everyday life. These are not prescriptive. They are meant to be applied to your life in whatever way you like or feel is best for you. In the end, I want you to have a life that belongs entirely to you, devoid of societal "shoulds" and built with your own desire and intuition. Everything in this part of the book leads you to more knowledge of yourself. These are concepts to master and learn, so you can learn more about you.

The tools shared in the next section of this book are meant to ease you on your journey, to help you discover more about yourself that will be generative to your happiness, healing, and growth.

I suspect some of them will resonate and some will take a little longer to apply to your life. That's okay. This is a journey. Your journey. May it continue to delight and surprise you.

CHAPTER 10

Be Intentional About Your Life

THIS IS A LOUD WORLD with a narrow definition of what it means to be successful. Success means being the best, and yet how can we *all* be the best? Success means building an empire, but if we're all dominating industries, where is the collaboration? Not everyone wants the stereotypical "big" life. And for many of us, we miss what we *actually* want, because we're so focused on what the world wants *from* us. Success, in its most conventional form, asks us to be impressive to others, to show off, to be better than someone else.

The answer is not to try to keep it all up, try to prove it all to others, try to dominate, try to grab at power. The answer is to opt out completely and consider your own definition of a successful, happy life.

What is *your* version of a big life? How do you define success? What makes you happiest? When do you feel most proud of yourself? Your freest life is not defined by someone else. It's not the life that is most glittery and exciting to other people. It's not a projection.

It's a life you live with awareness and intention.

What does it mean to live with intention? It means that whatever you're spending your time, money, and energy on is what you've actively chosen to have in your life. This may be a confronting thing to think about, especially if you feel mired in responsibility and obligation right now, but that's the beauty of starting to think more intentionally—you often realize how much of other people's "stuff" you've taken on. Friendships that feel more obligatory than fun or supportive. Responsibilities we've adhered to without ever thinking about it. Work that isn't fulfilling, but feels like the most realistic and practical choice. Taking our own choices away, simply because we haven't thought them through.

A fulfilling, purposeful, beautiful life does not happen by accident. It's a culmination of small, thoughtful steps taken consistently in the direction of what you most desire.

That's what an intentional life is about: identifying what you most genuinely want, not what you "should" want, not what society tells you to want, not what you think will prove you are so good at being good for everyone else. But, what *you* want. Maybe it's a comforting life in the country eating meals from your garden, with a pup at your side, letting go of huge, splashy ambitions you think you *should* have. Maybe it's moving to a big city, squeezing your belongings into a studio apartment, and taking the big ambitions you genuinely have seriously.

It doesn't matter *what* you want; it matters that you *listen* to yourself.

That you identify, for you, what you most want. Deeply. Truly. Authentically.

And then, that you don't stop there. You don't just sit around wanting it. You don't think about it and talk about it—you do it. Not to prove anything to anyone, but to honor yourself and your desires. To take what you want seriously. To love yourself through actions. Love is in the actions.

Think of a romantic relationship. Imagine your partner saying one thing and their actions lining up with another reality entirely. They *say* they love you, but they act in a way that doesn't really convey that sentiment.

The relationship you have with yourself is the exact same way. If you say you want something, truly, and then act in direct opposition to it, it creates an internal struggle. It creates dissatisfaction. It creates anxiety. It creates unhappiness.

When you align what you most want with your daily actions, something blooms within you. Something wonderful. Something joyful. You are listening to yourself.

Think of that same relationship—how it feels when that person says they love you and then acts in that way, holds your heart with tenderness and responsibility. Listens to you and cherishes what you have to say. Loves you with both their words and their actions. Doesn't it feel good?

That's how an intentional life feels.

Like you're listening to yourself and acting in accordance with that. Like you are showing yourself love, instead of just saying it.

Because, sticking to your word, creating habits that bolster consistency, and aligning what you want with an action plan is a radical act of self-love. It truly is. Because, what is love if not the word, the intent, and the action of being loving? Love cannot just be words alone. It cannot just be intent alone. It cannot just be action alone. It has to be all of it, together.

Maybe you want to start a business where you're the sole employee. Maybe you have no desire to build a team of twenty, sixty, a hundred in order to tell people that you've done it. Maybe you want to work just enough so you can live more. Maybe you want to paint in the evenings and never commercialize your art. Maybe you want your work hanging in galleries. Maybe you want a day job that pays the bills because you derive little satisfaction from work. Maybe you derive so much satisfaction from creative and artistic work that you need to create a life that serves it beautifully. Maybe you want kids. Maybe you want a dog that feels like a kid. Maybe you want a small house with a wraparound porch that makes you smile every time you sit there.

If you're so busy "keeping up" with what society says is valuable, you'll miss what will make you feel most satisfied. Doing more for the sake of doing more leads to resentment and burnout, and is ultimately less effective than doing less but with more intention.

The most practical way to be more intentional is to attach a tangible "why" to everything you are prioritizing and everything you're *not* prioritizing but feel like you "should" be prioritizing. Take meditation, for example. Everyone tells you that meditating is the gateway to a calmer life, right? But maybe meditation is not your thing. And so your "why" for meditating is: Other people told me to do it. This is not a strong enough why—and if you don't have a strong why, sticking with something becomes increasingly more difficult. Maybe you find cooking to be meditative. Maybe going on a walk in nature is meditative to you. When I go on a walk by the beach in Malibu, it puts me into a meditative and energetic state that I don't get from sitting on the ground listening to my breath for twenty minutes.

Everything you do, even the habits and rituals you think you "should" do, need to have a why. That is the basis of intention. You do things *on purpose*, as opposed to living on autopilot, trying to do enough and be enough in order to feel good. You construct a life that feels good on purpose, with your effort. When you live with intention, you'll end up doing a lot less, too. You don't need to wake up and journal for thirty minutes, meditate for twenty minutes, do yoga, write a gratitude journal, and make an elaborate green smoothie. Maybe you just do one thing that brings you calm in the morning and feels more purposeful because of its restraint.

Your why has to be something tangible and positive. You are *adding* something to your life. That's important. It's not about stopping something out of shame. Say you want to eat healthier. Focus the why on: "I love to eat healthier because when I do, I feel more clearheaded. I want to feel energized, so eating healthier foods will help that endeavor." As opposed to: "I hate my body, so I'm going to eat these 'healthy' foods I dislike."

Go toward the good, the positive outcome. Not just trying to outrun a shameful feeling, or to berate yourself. When you add things to your life for a good reason, you are ensuring your own success. Most times if you find yourself not sticking to something, it's likely because your why is constructed around shame. You're doing it because someone else told you to do it and you're trying to prove you can keep up. Or you're doing it to outrun a "negative" feeling, when instead you can do the same habit or action with a different intention—and the energy of it changes completely.

To this day, the reason I am so consistent with exercise is because I started to orient myself around a positive why. When my motivation would falter, I would remind myself: "Exercise makes me feel good. It gives me energy. It helps my mental health. I feel better whenever I exercise." And getting up to exercise feels a lot lighter, and I look forward to the positive benefit. I don't exercise because I hate my body, or because I feel like I must lose weight, or because it will make me feel "good enough." I exercise because it makes me feel healthy and energized throughout the day. Having a powerful and positive "why" helps me stay consistent in doing something I love and practicing a habit that brings me joy.

Being intentional with your time and attention is vital. It's the best antidote to feeling frantic, chaotic, and overwhelmed. It's also the best antidote to untangling yourself from the pressures of conventional success and that elusive need to "keep up." When you can pare down, simplify, and attach a positive "why" to whatever you're adding to your life, it all becomes a lot easier. And you end up adding actions to your life that directly benefit you and your well-being.

Go toward the good. Use your time with the intention that whatever you add is meant to help you feel good.

When you give yourself permission to opt out of the societal expectations, you get to find that voice within that is trying to create for you the most beautiful life that fits you perfectly. It may not *look* impressive, but it'll feel generative, lovely, and like home.

And who cares how it looks? How it *feels* is what matters. You being at home within the life you've consciously created. You living with freedom to change, to grow, to evolve, to reinvent.

It's *your* life.

It's allowed to be really, really good—on *purpose*.

CHAPTER 11

The Freedom of Consistency

REALISTICALLY, MOST OF US are not going to go off the grid and eschew modern life altogether. If you do, cool. That is not the life for me. Which means I've had to learn how to be an ambitious, creative person who doesn't put all her joy into some future where all my dreams come true. For one, that future doesn't exist. There will always be new challenges. Life isn't just *done*. It's not a to-do list, even though it's so often posited that way. I suspect you're like me in that you want to keep challenging yourself, but not to the point of burnout. Not just to prove you are worthy of your own life. But to feel the rewarding sense of accomplishment.

In order to do this, I've found that I must balance the pursuit with the enjoyment. Knowing when I've done enough for the day. And having a long-term vision for the pursuit that is open to flexibility and includes small celebrations along the way.

For this, discipline and consistency are the most freeing things to master. They may seem like just more tools of the productivity world, but actually they are our best defense against the endless and insatiable pursuit of more. Often, we can become angry with ourselves for not being where we expected to be in life, but if we are consistently putting in the steps toward a long-term endeavor and investing in ourself, then those feelings tend to fall away.

It's vital to keep our own promises. It's the cornerstone of a content life. Otherwise, things get out of balance. Most of us want a mix of enjoyment, pleasure, challenge, and pursuit. The priority level of each of these can change, but inevitably most people feel fulfilled when they have a mix and balance. It can't be all rest and no challenge. All pleasure and no pursuit. We are given desires for a reason. They don't have to be big or splashy, but if something deeply matters to you, the reward of being disciplined and consistent about bringing it to fruition is unparalleled. And it's a way outside the never-ending hustle culture mentality that is pushing us all to strive more.

Raw talent is the spark of any endeavor. But what makes the biggest difference—and is the most rewarding part of the journey—is being disciplined. It's surprising, because I always believed that discipline is strict, stringent, and based in shame. But actually I've found discipline to be intensely, intimately rewarding. Keeping promises to myself, regardless of how I might feel in the moment, means caring for my future self. I don't need external achievement to be happy, but when there are gifts inside of me that I want to bring into the tangible, the thing that works best to counteract the onslaught of hustle culture mentality is to focus on discipline. Consistency. Commitment.

Say you sit down to start a big endeavor that maybe you've never tried before. Of course, you're going to feel scared and doubtful. There's a big gap between where you are and where you're going. You've got to cross the bridge between your current skill and the skill you have to build up to. Whether it's with an artistic project or anything else, when you start something new, there's a gap between where you are and where you want to go. That fear convinces you that you will fail. You start comparing, feeling inadequate, contrasting your "lack" of progress with someone else's shiny success. And you give up. Your efforts trickle to a stop.

In order to keep your own promises, you have to be focused on cultivating something that isn't going to be dependent on how you "feel" on any given day. When you focus your efforts on being consistent, you don't worry about your motivations being fickle. You just know you have to keep up with your steps.

Consistency is the key that keeps us moving toward what we want. Think about it. When you do something consistently over time, you will see results. It may not be immediate, but results will happen. Decide to do one small thing every day or three times a week. Create a habit for yourself and keep at it. When you are consistent, you have the benefit of practice. There's a reason elite performers practice relentlessly. It's one thing to have raw talent, but it's another entirely to learn how to harness it, have it show up consistently, and be able to rely on it. I'm not saying you have to aspire to elite levels of anything, but there is something wonderfully generative about being consistent. You might think it's boring, but it's the complete opposite. You get to watch your talent flourish. You get to progress. You get to put in the effort and practice. It not only generates positive results in the tangible, but it also generates confidence, self-belief, and joy.

It doesn't even need to be huge strides forward. You can make significant progress on anything if you give it one hour per day of your time. Say you walk for an hour per day; think of where you'll be in a year. What used to feel impossible would feel easy.

Consistency is freeing. Weirdly. For a long time, I thought living in a habitual way would be boring and monotonous. You just do the same things every single day? *Why?* I'd rather be free and live my life every day as if it were my last. YOLO. Except I was certainly free in one way, but anxious in a lot of ways. Because each day wasn't *actually* my last. So, I was simply living without thinking of my future self at all. I gave my future self all of my burdens. I gave my future self a mess she would have to clean up. I gave my future self more complications.

Now, I think of my future self in a loving way. How can I make her life easier? How can I show up for her *now* so that the things I most want to do are in progress by the time they get to her? It's not about living in the future. It's about lovingly *preparing* for it.

I love habits, rituals, commitment, discipline, and consistency. They have saved my life. They have done more for releasing me from the grips of my anxiety than anything else. *Anything.*

Now, I give my future self the gift of progress.

I believe in starting with consistency over anything else. Whenever I start something new, I know I'm going to have the doubts. If I listen to the doubts, I'll give up. But instead of listening to the doubts, I focus entirely on building up a consistent routine and making sure all my efforts are small. Write for ten minutes per day, three times a week, for example. And I stick to that. I focus all my energy on just showing up for those ten minutes, three times a week. It doesn't matter if what I write completely sucks. It doesn't matter if it feels sticky and difficult and progress comes in spurts. I am simply building the momentum of consistency. I am building the muscle of showing up.

If you keep going, if you focus on being consistent over being perfect, it all adds up. And you stop worrying about being "good enough" and instead get excited about new levels of that talent and skill. You start to rely on that talent. You don't have to wait for inspiration or until you're "ready." You show up, and the readiness builds.

The thing about being stuck in the spirals is that we don't always want to be found. Our comfort zone can often become sadness, the edge of depression, the pervasive buzz of anxiety. This can feel like safety. To not have hope for change. If we don't have hope, if we don't try, if we don't give anything a shot, if we let self-doubt determine our possibilities—then we can't be disappointed.

But I learned there's a different kind of disappointment.

The kind that is borne from inaction.

And that is the kind that crystallizes into regret.

Many of us try to *think* our way out of self-doubt. We wait to be more ready, as if there's some future version of us that has the nerve to believe in ourself. That's part of why we try to collect so much achievement and approval. We hope that it adds up enough that we finally sink into an impenetrable self-belief.

But I've come to understand that self-doubt and self-belief do not work this way at all. The nerve has to come from the showing up. The confidence has to be earned, built, and cultivated. Confidence does not come from a thought, from thinking our way into it, from waiting until we "feel" confident.

Confidence comes from action.

Which is a concept I was extremely averse to for a long time. I kept thinking if I could just get my mind on board with my skill level, then I'd be good. If only I could believe that everyone else thought I was good enough, then I would be good enough. But confidence does not come from some external approval. I let myself think that if enough people believed in me, then I could believe in myself. So I waited. Waited until it accumulated.

Until I stopped waiting. Because it just never accumulated. I never felt "ready" or "good enough."

I bought a planner at the beginning of 2016 in the rush of heady excitement about the new year being "my year." It came with a sticker that I planted on the bottom left corner of my desktop iMac. The sticker said: "Action cures fear." I liked the idea that there could be a cure to fear. It was theoretical at first.

Until I started taking action more and more, on the things that were most important to me—and felt fear dissipate, as if it hadn't ever existed. The more action I took and the less I tried to think my way into a "fix," the more I realized the vital importance of getting out of my head and into my life.

When I made a spreadsheet of all the debt I owed, fear lessened. When I made the outline for my first digital course, my fear percentage went down. When I started posting on Instagram more and caring about metrics less, fear had nowhere to flourish within me. The more I write, the less I fear. The more I exercise, the less I worry about not showing up for myself. The more I honor my own promises to myself, the more confident, trustworthy, and held I feel.

Action cures fear, and it also does a lot more than that. It builds confidence. It builds your self-belief. It creates trust within you. It's a generator, in that sense. When you honor your own promises, you teach yourself that you are reliable, that you won't abandon yourself.

Think of it this way: In all our relationships, especially romantic ones, we say that actions speak louder than words. Now, wouldn't that apply to the relationship we have with ourselves? Actions speak louder than words.

When you show up for yourself—in action—you generate belief. You generate your own love. You know you can rely on yourself. You know you have your own back.

And guess what happens when you know you can rely on, trust, and believe in yourself?

Magic.

If there's something you really want to do, and it comes from a genuine place, make a list of the small steps it will take to get there. Then, make an actionable and realistic plan for completing those small steps. Let the steps be really small. Let the momentum of progress build. You don't have to do everything at once. Just make sure you are building up the action muscle, that you are building up consistency and discipline.

Then, complete those small steps. Commit to yourself. And celebrate every single time you complete the small steps. You might think it's overkill, but you are training yourself to care about the small wins. And every big endeavor needs to have a collection of small wins. It's what keeps us going. Be proud of yourself.

When you start taking action, instead of keeping all your best ideas inside of you, trapped, waiting to be "ready," you stop looking *out there* for the very thing you are meant to give *yourself*.

That sense of pride in completing the small steps and taking action despite feeling afraid—there's nothing like it.

Another added benefit of consistency is that you stop worrying as much about the results. The staying consistent, the progress, the effort—it becomes something redeeming all its own. It feels like the gift. It's not boring at all. It's exciting. It almost becomes more exciting than the thing you were trying to achieve. Because that effort belongs to you. It's something *you've* built. Commitment and consistency can generate so much positive momentum in your life.

If there's something that you genuinely want to add to your life, that you've had a hard time adding because of fear, just remember: Anything new will have the gap. The self-doubt is a part of it. It's telling you that you're doing something new. It doesn't mean you're not good enough, or talented enough. That's the fear talking.

The best thing you can do for yourself is get that plan of small steps together. Start tiny. Tinier than you think. I promise it'll build up. And it will build up even faster than you can imagine. Once you can put aside the clawing need to be "good enough" right away, you can focus on practice. You can focus on your effort. You can focus on being consistent.

And once you have the consistency down, you will not even believe the way your life can open up. Lost dreams will come back to you. New aspirations will present themselves. And you'll be fascinated by what it takes to build up the effort, make the progress, and instill the positive momentum necessary to get where you want to go. And that progress will be the gift. It really will.

The antidote to waiting to be "good enough" is to stack up the days. Put in the progress. Get consistent. Make a commitment that is nonnegotiable. Carve out the time. And show up for yourself.

Showing up for yourself will generate so much joy, you almost won't believe it.

Just try it.

You'll see.

CHAPTER 12

The Beauty of Experimentation

THERE'S A MYTH A LOT OF US like to believe in. It's the idea that if we were there, in someone else's success, we'd be happy. Like if we had technology to trade places with someone we perceive as doing "better" than us, then all will be well, all ills would be cured, and we'd never have a moment of pain or insecurity ever again. It's the love-hate dichotomy of celebrity at work. You want to be them, but you also hate them for having a life that appears to be better than your own.

But we miss something important here. One, not everyone who has that kind of success is happy. It's not a 1 + 1 logical equation. I've come to understand that if you're not ready to receive your success, it hurts more than it helps. What I mean is, if you're feeling undeserving of success, or you have placed that kind of success on a pedestal, thinking it will solve all your "issues," then it's going to amplify all the things you were trying to run away from.

Two, receiving and allowing are a lot more difficult than you might think. You may think, okay, but I wouldn't have to do any mind-set or healing work because then I'd be rich and famous. It's why people are always surprised when a rich and famous person takes their own life. "But they had everything!" Yeah, but they probably bought into all the same ideas as everyone else. That once they're rich and famous and beloved, they'll be happy and all their emotional demons will fall away. And when they get there, maybe they recognize that nothing falls away, that fame and money don't do anything except amplify where they're most broken and hurting, and now they have to keep up the facade as the perfect rich and famous person everyone expects them to be, otherwise they're ungrateful. And also, they so wanted that money and fame to solve their problems and now that it hasn't? Despair.

A lot of us have a hard time, even in our non-famous lives, accepting and receiving happiness of any kind. A lot of us don't know how to feel good. It's why Americans accumulate so much. We think money is happiness. So, of course people are going to overspend, overexert, and put all their hopes and dreams on becoming richer—that's what we've been told *is* happiness.

Now I'm not saying that someone living in poverty wouldn't be 100 percent happier and safer if they had a living wage. I don't blame anyone for being in poverty. But that's a moral issue, that we are a rich, developed country and still let our people live in poverty or unhoused. I don't want to go off on that tangent, but it feels important to call out.

That being said, once you realize that getting to some external place isn't going to bring you the healing and happiness you think it will, your life can open up in new ways. If you are unable to receive happiness exactly where you are, receiving it when you're at some pinnacle of career success isn't likely to happen either. That doesn't mean you tamp down your ambition. It simply means you redirect your efforts. People think that they can skate by the inner work if they accumulate and achieve enough. There are lots of people living in big houses who are not happy. Who are isolated. Who are unkind to others. Who are abusing drugs and alcohol. Who are connected only to their bank accounts, their things, their possessions. I like nice things. I do. But they go in their rightful place, as something fun to enjoy, not as my entire worth as a human being.

Fame can be a burden. Having the kind of conventional and splashy success we're told to want can also be a burden. But we assume these are universal goods. That nobody could possibly be unhappy if they are rich and famous. And if we believe that about strangers we'll likely never meet, how does that affect the way we think about ourselves?

You have to be ready to receive blessings. This idea that more is always better is a myth. We miss out on seeing how fulfilled we could be with less. We miss out on our own lives entirely, by trying to receive what isn't meant for us.

You need to find your own version of greatness. Maybe you really will become a famous actor. Or maybe you'll start a business creating cool logos for people. I don't know. But don't let what's meant for you miss you because you're so focused on it being better. So focused on other people who you think have it better than you.

Get ready to receive what's meant for you. Receive your own happiness first. Try that on for a while. Then see what dreams and aspirations flourish from there. Value that. Value yourself. Value your own life. Stay in your unique lane.

All of us are meant for greatness, but that greatness is going to look very different for each of us. And that's okay. That's how it's meant to be.

We are so serious about things. So serious. We are told that we need to pick a path, strive for that path, and never, ever give up, quit, or change direction. And if we don't get to wherever we thought we were supposed to be—a path we chose—we are meant to feel like failures and disappointments.

But, what if you just . . . tried things?

I know.

A monumental question.

What if you got experimental with your life? What if you stopped trying to create meaning from every little detour, redirection, rejection, or shift—and instead embraced it? What if you could trust that you were being led to something even better than you could imagine, if only you could let go of the image you have in your mind of how it's "supposed" to go?

What if you simply experimented?

Say you want to make music. That's your thing. You've wanted to sing and write songs since you were younger. But, because you think it needs to be a Whole Thing and you don't know how you're going to make money from it and you have no idea if you're even any good or if you even absolutely love it and what if you're not "good enough," whatever "good enough" means . . . ? Okay, so you spend years building up the *idea* of making music. The less you do of it, the more you build it up. It becomes an impossible task. A burden. If you're not going to be the world's best musician, why even do it? If you can't make a full-time living from your music, why even try? Now it's become a resentment. A regret. Proof of failure.

And yet . . . you haven't even *written* many songs.

You've lived an entire creative career in your mind.

Because of that intense pressure to *know*. You have to know whether it'll "work out." You have to know whether you'll be "successful."

But what if you just stopped caring about it working out or being successful? What if you simply experimented with your music? What if you put it into practice with absolutely zero expectations and pressure? What if you did it for the joy of it? What if you wrote music and sang and played your instruments as often as possible because you *like* it?

Maybe you realize that making music for a career will kill the joy of it. The dream is not always commercializing your art. Take it from someone who spent a year writing clickbait articles, thinking that was the ultimate dream in becoming a Real Writer, when in actuality it killed my soul and joy for a long time.

Maybe songwriting and singing is meant to be your release. Your hobby. A thing you do that doesn't have to *be* anything for you.

Or maybe you realize that actually you don't like writing music that much. In your mind, it seemed a lot more exciting than in reality. So, maybe you realize that it wasn't so much about the music, *exactly*, but the feeling of being creative. Maybe you get a microphone and start a podcast. Maybe you start doing voiceover work. Maybe you start a freelance side business that becomes a full-time business. Maybe that creativity was meant to channel somewhere else.

Or maybe you become a famous singer. And your songs make it onto the radio.

Whatever happens, you'll never know if you don't experiment and try new things.

If you don't get the "what if" out of your head and into the world.

Give things a shot. Try. Be experimental with life. Isn't this all one big experiment anyway? Isn't your life unprecedented, the way you have no idea where you'll land, how long you'll be on this Earth? All of life is an experiment.

You can either fight it.

Or embrace it.

It's a hell of a lot more fun if you embrace it.

Try it out.

Have a ball.

CHAPTER 13

Release the Need for Control

WE WORRY, WE STRESS, and we activate our anxiety trying to control the future. A future that is, by nature, uncertain. But in that uncertainty, we try to make these lavish plans. This is how it will go. This is how life will work for me. This is what will make me happy. We make the lists, and the plans, and then become stressed and disappointed when our plans don't go to plan.

When we didn't even need to make the lavish plan in the first place.

It stems from one very particular place: the idea that we know exactly what will make us happy and if only we could get it, we'd be better off.

So, that place becomes a utopia in our minds—somewhere to escape to when the mundanity of daily life gets to be too much. It becomes a destination, something tangible we think is out there. And we project all our future calm onto it. I'm only anxious because I'm not there yet. Why aren't I there yet? Some other people are there, so that must mean *I've* fallen behind. I need to catch up. I need to do more. I need to get back into my hustle. I can't stop. I can't rest. I can't ever relax. I *have* to get there. Because when I get there, I'll be okay. I'll be worthy. I'll have caught up. I'll be keeping up with everyone else. Once I'm there, I can be happy knowing I didn't fail the game of life. I kept up. I caught up. I'll be *good*.

But where did this idea of "there" come from? What is the destination? What meaning have we given that future? And how do we know that once we arrive we'll even enjoy any of it?

I've spent my life constructing daydreams and fantasies and plans, entire worlds that felt safe and comfortable, an external projection of my future that I felt could inure me to pain and disappointment. I've spent a lot of time staring off into an unpromised horizon, hoping that one day my life would get better. And I've made a lot of plans, based on my age, my experience, what I felt was owed to me, what I thought "should" have happened already. I've used other people's lives as a barometer for my own. If it happened for them and didn't happen for me, that must mean I'm not as good as them. That's the formula I used.

Because of this formula, I've created an unnecessary flurry of anxious energy in my life. I've spent so much time being stressed. I've been worried that things were not going to work out the way I expect them to. And I have exacerbated my own stress simply because I made a plan and got frustrated that the plan I fabricated in my mind wasn't working out exactly how I expected it to.

I wrote a novel in 2020. I had a plan of what I was going to do with it. I'd send it to my agent at the time, she'd get a book deal for me, and then I'd write a novel a year. I constructed this plan without any experience. I decided that was how it was going to go, and then I got really, really, really controlling about it. I started to resent the work I had to do to make money while I wrote on the side. I started to feel a panic building in me that I was "behind" and had to "catch up." I decided that I *needed* to be a novelist. That it would fulfill me. That it was what I'd been missing.

How quickly the control snuck in. I didn't want to clench around it, but it happened anyway. I didn't fully trust myself yet. There was still a part of me that wanted to wrench my way into the life I expected.

Because I had been such an impulsive free spirit in the past and had worked so hard to change the trajectory of that life, I went to the other extreme. Instead of being a free spirit, I'd become controlling. I wouldn't let myself be spontaneous, because my spontaneity had led me into situations that I didn't want to find myself back in. I thought being in control was an important part of my evolution.

I sent the novel to my agent at the time. My anxiety spiked. I was terrified of what she was going to say. And when she replied that she didn't think the book was ready, I felt the anger of my plan being taken from me. I was *invested* in that imaginary, yet ironclad plan. And here was the first big hurdle to it.

I kept thinking: *This isn't how it was supposed to go.* It was causing me a lot of harm. And then, one weekend, I realized, I am the one causing my own harm here. It was my addiction to the plan that was making me frustrated. It was my own projected time line of this novel that was causing me the most anxiety.

I believed in that novel. I believed in my own resiliency. And I decided to do something that many people told me not to do. I broke up with my agent. I let go of the grasp I had on my plan and my control. I told myself, *If I'm meant to be a novelist, if I'm meant to get a novel out in the world, then it will happen. It will happen the way it's meant to happen.* It was a presumption of faith I hadn't quite embodied yet. But it was a person I wanted to be. I didn't want to still be tied to outcomes, to plans, to it all working out exactly as I needed it to be. I can be shortsighted. I don't always see the whole picture. I don't have a bird's-eye view of my life. Maybe something better was on the horizon. Maybe something I couldn't predict or plan was on its way to me. Maybe I could trust that.

A couple of weeks after I broke it off with my agent, I sent my novel to a few other literary agencies. I didn't edit the novel. I just wanted to see what would happen. It felt important to send it out to a few places. Not hundreds of agencies, but a few. Just to see.

And in the waiting, I worked to divest myself from the outcome of that novel. I worked to divest myself from all my outcomes. How it performs. What people think. I worked to trust that what was meant for me, would be. And that I will take inspired action when I am led to do so. I had to stop trying to force it all.

A few months later, I signed with my top choice literary agency and with an agent who fell in love with my novel. That decision to let go of the control led me right back to the dream, but in a totally different way. Now, I'm just excited to see where my writing takes me. No clenching. No forcing. No plans. It will be what it will be.

That is my new mantra: It will be what it will be.

And also: Whatever's meant for me, will be.

I don't want a plan. I don't want control. I want to let life surprise me. I want to be in the right place at the right time, always. I want my life to be synchronicities. I want to be led. I want to hear my intuition and find myself in the exact place I'm meant to be. I only want what's meant for me. I only want alignment. I want it all to unfold better than I could imagine. Better than my plans. More magical. More interesting. More exciting.

Our need to control all the outcomes in our lives limits our possibilities.

Control can be cunning in this way. It gives us the idea that we can actually control the way things unfold for us. For a lot of us, we feel safe in claiming control. But what I have come to understand is that our "plans" are usually based in only two things: 1) What you see other people have and think that you should want; and 2) Your past and what you think is possible for yourself. Neither of those things is expansive. Control limits how good it could be.

Letting go of control is about holding on to a rough vision of your life, but keeping yourself open to all the detours, to the intuitive nudges. We so often end up comparing ourselves to others, and those comparisons lead us to try to control our own life, thinking we need it all to look a certain way. But if we stay open, if we listen within, if we follow our own unique path, we end up needing control a lot less. When we're trying to control, it usually means we're comparing. We're in the "should." Change the expectation. Change the meaning of that outcome. When we recognize that we cannot earn our own worth, control seems a lot less appealing.

I used to think that if I could clench down, make a plan, and stick to it, then it will all work out the way I think will make me happiest. Which put me in the precarious position of needing it all to work out the way I expect and feeling disappointed when it inevitably does not. Because, when it doesn't work out, we tend to create stories about why. It must mean we're failing, or not good enough, or some other trigger of an insecurity from our past. When, in actuality, maybe it didn't work out because it wasn't *meant* to work out. And if we can stop ourselves from making a story about what it not working out means, then we'll be able to stay focused enough to see it all work out even better.

Because we clench around control, we make ourselves think that we actually *do* know how it's going to work out. But that idea of how it works out is based on someone else's experience. It's usually born from comparison, that we need to keep up with this checklist of societal expectations. But if we can resist the checklist, we can live from a much more genuine place.

We actually don't know how it's all going to unfurl for us. We think we know how we'll get from point A to point Z, but we have no idea. And maybe we don't even want to get to point Z. Maybe we're supposed to be doing something entirely differently—and we miss the detours.

The beauty of letting go of control is that you aren't stuck in the anxiety spiral of how your plan was supposed to go. You get to enjoy the process of being completely outside the bounds of your plan. It's better on the other side. It's not unsafe. It's wonderful. Because whatever comes to you feels like it's uniquely meant for you. If you don't have to force it all to happen, you get to experience the magic of it happening. If you can get beyond the plans and control and time lines and how it's going for someone else and how it's not going for you, then you can click into alignment with all the things that are trying to get to you. The partners that will make you feel inspired. The opportunities that will fit you like a glove. The experiences that will activate your joy, not your anxiety. The "I didn't expect it to happen this way, but I'm so glad it did" moments.

I don't need to prove anything by how busy or in demand I am. My life is not for consumption. That means I can wait for what aligns. I don't have to be frantic. It can all unfold slower than the pace of the world. I don't make that *mean* anything about how good I am (or not).

The aligned moments are the *only* moments I want now. I only want it if I light up. That is the standard. My skin better buzz from the inside out. It's a *hell yes* or it's a definite no.

Trying to bend everything to your own will creates anxiety, not diffuses it. That's what I mistakenly believed—that controlling everything, making the plans, will lessen anxiety. But that's not how it works. Trying to keep everything controlled not only makes us miss what's meant for us, but it also makes us *more* worried, panicked, and stressed.

We are a generation wracked by anxiety. We do so much to try to avoid that anxiety. We control. We give up on our dreams. We overdo harmful behaviors. We harm ourselves, all trying to distract from that anxiety.

I've learned to make friends with my anxiety, to recognize that it's trying to serve me in some way. I listen to it. I genuinely ask: What are you trying to tell me? Most times, it's trying to let me know that I am grasping too hard at trying to control everything, that I have put my current mood in the hands of some future outcome, that I am not living in the present.

As with anything else, making friends with your emotions can lessen their impact. Listen to what they are trying to tell you. Emotions are not to be feared, even though we live in a society that makes it seem that way. Emotions are tools; they give us information that will allow us to know ourselves better. If we are too busy distracting from our anxiety, controlling every moment and thinking our lives will be "fixed" at some future point, we're missing the wisdom of right now, the very thing our emotions are trying to tell us to pay attention to.

I never thought I'd one day be happy that my plan didn't work out, but I am now. I am so glad those opportunities missed me. I'm so happy I didn't force it to happen. I'm so happy I didn't bend and break and contort to make it all work out the way I thought it should.

I'm so happy I ended up here. Free of the plans. Free of control. And just positively expecting that whatever is meant for me will make itself known.

Relax.

What's coming is better than your plans.

CHAPTER 14

Cultivate Real Self-trust

I SOMEWHAT RESENT the commercialization of self-love and self-care. It's become A Lot. It's become a loud advertising promotion, and yet neither of those things can be presented in pretty, pink packaging. There is no self-love if there isn't first self-hate. And self-hate is not pretty. There is no self-care if there isn't first self-abandonment. We've packaged these up as face masks and bubble baths, but in actuality, they are a violent unbecoming. A violent unlearning within a violent society. Not to get too radical about it.

But let's get radical.

And let's be real. Self-care only needs to exist in the way that it does because we aren't taught or encouraged to care for ourselves. To care for others, either. Or, if we're taught to care for others, it's done sacrificially. We either care too much for others and not enough for ourselves, or we risk looking selfish to others, who think we shouldn't need to care for ourselves. It's a lose-lose. There is a reason we need self-care, and that's because we have learned to self-neglect.

And there's a reason we need self-love. Because we are stuck in the whirlwind of a culture that does not want us to love ourselves. When we love ourselves, we stop buying fixes. We stop thinking we are someone in need of being fixed and bettered—at all times. And that is not good for business. Our self-hatred, self-loathing, self-doubt—these are lucrative to lots and lots of companies. The same companies that are now trying to capitalize on the "trend" of self-love and self-care. The same magazines that created the beauty and life standards that have birthed a culture of women who don't know how to love themselves now want to give you the top five products you can buy to have a #Self-Care Sunday.

What bullshit.

Real self-love is not pretty. It's healing in a way that means you have to face all the things you've been avoiding. It's not staring into the mirror and telling yourself five things you like about yourself. (Well, it's not *only* that.) It's having to look at a culture that hasn't loved you back. It's having to unlearn why you started hating yourself in the first place. It's disillusionment. It's grief. It's waking up to a reality you've been trying to stay asleep to. It's not a meadow of wildflowers. It's a hurricane.

Maybe some self-care can be soft and gentle. I love that kind of self-care. But the real self-care that changed me were not the shiny, sexy things. It was getting out of debt, getting myself an exercise routine I didn't hate, eating in a way that didn't punish my body, and setting up and committing to the habits and rituals that actually bring mental wellness. A face mask doesn't really do any of that for me. Self-care is much deeper, quieter.

And to me, self-care is more about self-trust.

More than a lack of love, a lack of care, women have a lack of trust in themselves. We care about other people's opinions over our own opinion. We follow the societal "shoulds." We hate our body because it doesn't live up to some impossible standard. We grow up in an environment that does not want us to trust ourselves. Women who trust themselves are dangerous, unruly, and uncontrollable. They will not be obedient, acquiescent, or suppressed.

Self-trust is a personal revolution. And it's built the same way any other trust is built. It's earned. You have to keep your promises to yourself. You have to really listen to your own needs. You have to stop suppressing your emotions—and, instead, hear them. You have to learn how to turn off the noise of the world, and find the still, quiet whisper of your own intuition. You have to opt out of whatever is dulling you, whatever is unhealthy for you, and replace it with something generative and kind and peaceful.

When you trust yourself, you hold yourself.

Self-love is about seeing yourself as worthy, regardless of where you're at in life.

Self-care is the act of love.

Self-trust is knowing the difference between what's real within, and what has been programmed into you.

There's a lot of advice out there. A lot of books (including this one). A lot of podcasts. A lot of articles. A lot of influencers, experts, and people with authority. There is so much out there to consume, offline and online. But at the end of the day, what really matters is how you feel. Do you need to take someone else's advice? Does it feel right to you? Does it light you up?

Discernment is the foundation of self-trust. You need it in a loud, dissatisfied world. Our brains are naturally porous, able to process information quickly—and yet, on the internet for example, that porousness can actually be a detriment. We are scrolling fast, consuming the words and opinions of others without much discernment.

Many times I've been scrolling through my social media feed

only to walk away feeling a tightness in my stomach, a pinch of shame, without knowing where it even originated from. Just some post I read that made me feel inadequate or insecure or question myself.

Maybe I consumed some person's life that was meant to be aspirational, selling me their interiors, skin care, and makeup, and I felt like I wasn't measuring up. I used to think I would have to make someone like that "wrong" so that my way could be "right." We call this judgment. And it hurts more than it heals.

We don't need more judgment in this world, though. I don't need to make another person wrong for myself to be right. I don't need to add hate to this world, or to hate-follow anyone, or hate-read anything. We can be critical and hold people account-able for wrongdoings, but when we judge, we are putting each other on this invisible hierarchy, the same hierarchy that is harming us all. The same hierarchy that is measuring us. It's not necessary to contribute to that.

What we need in a noisy, frantic, endlessly dissatisfied, bloated with excess world is: discernment.

Discernment is a master class in self-trust. I can watch another woman's life on Instagram now and not try to make her wrong. That is her path. Her journey. She's done the work to find what lights her up—and who am I to say she shouldn't have that?

I can watch her life and take the pieces that feel valuable and relevant to me. I can discern between what's for me and what isn't—without lobbing a judgment at her. What we judge in others we judge in ourselves. And I spent so much time not being discerning that I learned to judge others on successes they may have had before me, which meant that I judged myself whenever I got to that level. I judged my desires, without discerning what's for me and what's not.

Discernment in the online world is vital. It's a lot to consume. A lot of lives to watch. A lot of celebrations and highlight reels. A lot of advice. So much advice.

Discernment brings the power back to you. You listen within. You ask yourself if this lines up with what you value and believe. If you get triggered, you're tasked to heal something within. Without discernment, it's all too easy to become lost, confused, overwhelmed, and weighed down by comparison online. You'll find yourself wanting something you never cared about before, maybe overspending to get it, or being upset with yourself that you don't have it. Or you'll want someone else's achievement, or want to live their way of life, which takes you out of your own unique experience. This is your life. Take in advice as needed, but remember that it comes down to you. What lights you up? What feels true *to* you? What feels right *for* you? Discernment helps you know the difference.

I can't tell you what a radically content life will look or feel like for you. We're all unique. The expectation that we should want the same exact things, look the exact same way, and desire to have the exact same kind of life—where is the fun in that? I don't want you to follow *my* path. I want you to carve out your own. Build your own life. Feel as though whatever you do is like a home within the global home. That you've come home to yourself.

I want you to know your truth. And curate, create, and build a life that is yours. That you can belong to. At the end of everything, that, to me, is living a radically content life. Because it's yours. You don't need it to look a certain way. You don't need to prove anything to anyone. You're not keeping up with others. It's you doing you—wonderfully, happily, contentedly.

Discernment pares down the information. Discernment gives you the initial tool. Knowing what is *not* for you is just as important as knowing what *is* for you. There's less to care about. Less to try to "get." Discernment allows you to care fiercely about what you truly want to care about.

This is your life. I'm going to keep reminding you of that because we so often forget it. Your life. It is your task to make it as joyful, happy, wonderful, generative, as you wish. That is your infinite power.

I've come to understand that self-trust may have the greatest importance of all. It's the foundation. It's difficult to love someone you don't trust. And it's difficult to care for someone you don't love. Self-trust, then, becomes the ground on which these other states of being stand. Self-trust is the beginning. And it's often the one part we skip over.

So, how do you build up self-trust?

Honor how you feel and find a way to tell the truth to yourself. To *yourself*. You don't have to say it out loud. But there is no trust without the truth. And we do a good job of concealing even our own truth from ourselves. Maybe you start journaling. That's the easiest, most direct way. Start telling the truth. Start with: "How am I feeling today?" And stop being afraid of your truth. It might seem scary to name the fears, the worries, the insecurities, but naming them and letting them hit the open air is freeing.

You need to release the pressure valve within.

You need to start saying what you actually mean—even if it's to *yourself* first. The trust in yourself erodes when you act in direct opposition to how you feel. When you keep suppressing what is trying to be expressed. When you keep ignoring what is calling to you. When you sacrifice your own truth, thinking that's what the world expects of you. When you curve yourself around someone else, without being your own whole self first. When you take another person's opinion of you as truth, even if it's not how you really feel about yourself.

When you abandon yourself—and call it love.

So, the first step to self-trust is to stop abandoning yourself. Start listening within. Start hearing yourself.

Then you get to know your needs. What is it that you need to be happily yourself?

And you can start taking care of your real needs.

That's self-care.

Giving yourself what you need.

Self-trust identifies what you really need, the real you, the uncovered you, the maskless you.

Self-care provides.

And from the trust, from the care, comes the love.

You can feel safe to heal. You have a foundation to heal from.

You trust yourself to hold yourself. You hear your pain—and you honor it. You care for it. You cradle it.

Self-love is the expression of that. The eventuality.

Maybe you've tried to go from zero to self-love. Maybe you've tried to bubble bath your way into feeling held. Maybe you've found yourself more lost in the impossible maze of commercialized self-love. Maybe these words sound like white noise to you now.

Everything starts with trust.

If we can't hold ourselves, we can't hold anything else.

Hold yourself.

CHAPTER 15

Let Life Be Easy on You

THIS IS A HARSH, DEMANDING, complicated world full of contradictions and corruptions. It's hard enough sometimes just to be alive. It can weigh on a heart just to have to witness the world as it is. Which is why I think you need to be your own best friend, the softest place to land for yourself. It's one thing to be compassionate toward the world; it's another to be its martyr. You can only give as much as you give to yourself. You need to fill yourself up, too. Remember that when you are trying to save everyone else, you have to save yourself first.

Life is not a race. When we buy into the ways of the world, it's always about keeping up. And if we are constantly worried about keeping up, we won't give ourselves the space and time to heal, rest, and enjoy the life we've built. We won't stop to listen to our emotions, our intuitive nudges, anything at all, if we're trying to keep up with a fast-paced world that thrives on instant gratification.

Healing is not a quick fix. So, sleep. Care for your health. Take breaks. Take your vacations. You are not meant to be in pursuit at every moment. Let yourself actually enjoy your achievements, how far you've come. Celebrate the healing you've done the same way you celebrate the material gains. Be your own fiercest advocate. Trust that your own love, and your own joy, is leading you to beautiful and surprising places.

Let life be easy on you for a while. Live lightly. This world can be very difficult, but please don't be your own biggest barrier. Don't be the person who tells you that you can't do it, or it's too late, or you're too old. You can do it. It's not too late. And age does not tell you what's possible for you. Wherever you are now, you can be in a totally different place a month, a year from now. So much can change when you stay open. When you stay hopeful. Stop resisting life and the changes it wants from you. Let life take you on the tide for a while. See where you go when you stop getting in your own way. See all that is available for you when you're open to a transformation.

Learning how to be compassionate toward yourself doesn't happen overnight. And it doesn't have to. Becoming even more truer and freer versions of yourself is rewarding. It's enough. Everything else is simply decoration.

Remember to live. It's important to heal, to be aware of how you interact with your thoughts, but also . . . life is here to be lived. Experiment. Trust yourself to go out into the world and be able to handle whatever comes at you. Walk on shaky legs. Don't get so stuck in your mind that you then start waiting to be fully healed in order to live. Take up a journaling habit so you always know where to go when you're overwhelmed, confused, anxious, or lost. Tell the truth to yourself. Let it live outside of you. Don't be afraid of your emotions. They are signals, signs, communications. A whole world of transformation and magic opens to you when you can sit with your emotions instead of scratch away at them, escape them, distract them, or disassociate from them. Your feelings are wisdom. They just want to be heard. Start writing down your feelings. Start facing yourself. Start going out into the world bravely, and know you can always come home to you.

Be your own safe space. It's a lot easier to let other people support you when you support yourself. You are not an island, but you are your own home. It's important you make that home as lovely and beautiful as you can. It's important that your mind becomes a place that makes you feel good, that you can return to for encouragement. It's nice to get all that from others, but it's something else entirely to get it from yourself.

Grow. And evolve. Become so many different versions of yourself. Outgrow who you used to be. Try and fail. Learn. And unlearn. Peel back more layers.

Let your awareness lead to action. Act and live from a healed state. Unlearn so you can live with more freedom, not so you can become a perpetual self-improvement project. You have to get out into the world and live, too. You have to expose yourself to new experiences and trust that you will have your own back. That you will be there for you, no matter what happens. Be the unconditional love in your life. Be the nonjudgmental person in your life. Be the person in your life that says: Let's live boldly and bravely.

Life is a series of healing. You are never "done." It's not a destination to arrive at. It's an unfolding. A becoming. A tightening up to loosen again.

That's how it works. You live, you uncover a layer, you are asked to go deeper, and you sink into a part of you that feels even more true than the person you were a year, a month, a week, a minute before. In many ways, it's about shedding what holds you back from experiencing your life as it's happening. Healing will not be linear. It will not arrive one day in perfect form. Stop trying to be "done" with the work of becoming yourself. Stop rushing it. You have a lifetime to master it. You're meant to have a lifetime to become, unfold, tense, and unfold again. It all belongs. It's all part of it. Maybe you need a break once in a while, but don't quit becoming truer versions of yourself. You don't have to become "better." Just truer. More you. More expressed. More free.

Let life come at you. Ride the ride. Be alive to it all. Every single thing. It could all work out for you. Maybe it's already finding a way to work out for you. Be in the balance of life, the flow. Do the work, then let the work speak for itself. Accept what is and change what you can't accept. Make a plan, have a vision, then stay open to the magic of the plan completely changing. Life wants your trust.

When you give it, all you'll see are possibilities.

CHAPTER 16

Write New Narratives for Yourself

EACH OF US HAS A STORY we repeat to ourselves, based on how we interpreted the events of our past and how we translate our current situation. This is all perception, for the most part. Your identity is not fixed. Your story is not fact. Whatever happened to you, the pain of it is caused by your interpretation of the event. That's not to say that people shouldn't be held accountable for harm, but that we have to be responsible for the way we synthesize our personal histories. What we make our past mean. Who we *believe* we are is who we are.

And "belief" is mutable and flexible. Which means we can change our beliefs about ourselves. We can rewrite our stories. We can create new narratives. We can teach our minds to see ourselves in a totally different light.

I didn't believe this was possible until I did it with surprising success. There was so much about my past that I interpreted in a negative way, harming myself with my own harshness. What I made my past mean is what I brought into my current reality. And I was so certain about my identity—that I'd never be able to change, or be habitual, or not be self-destructive or self-loathing. I didn't think I'd *ever* be a happy person. I thought I'd live my entire life self-sabotaging all the good and making it mean I was undeserving.

If you find yourself stuck in this fixed identity, I want you to try this powerful exercise. It takes only ten to fifteen minutes per day and it can change how you view yourself. It's like putting on a whole new filter through which to see your life. It will open your eyes to how much your happiness depends on how you interpret and translate the events that happen to you. Do you interpret your life in a negative bent? Are you prone to assuming the worst?

What you focus on is what expands in your life. If you focus your thinking on being affirming, loving, compassionate, and uplifting, then wouldn't it track that your life will follow suit? That you will interpret your everyday interactions and situations through the lens of an affirming mind?

I love this ritual so much I call it the Magical Thinking Ritual.

Because it's creating magical thoughts, which lead to magical actions, which lead to magical situations, which lead to a magical life. It all starts in your thoughts.

And instead of having to change your external environment to change your perception, try changing your perception, which will change how you view your external environment.

The Magical Thinking Ritual is based on writing positive affirmations every single day. Affirmations are encouraging words you can say or write to yourself. There's a few reasons why this actually works, and it's not about bypassing very real emotions.

I think affirmations are somewhat polarizing.

Rightfully so, there is a backlash against toxic positivity. I agree with that backlash. I am always here for the full spectrum of emotions. Writing affirmations and training the mind to expect the positive doesn't mean we ignore our emotions that come up. It means that we are better poised to be able to listen to those emotions, because we aren't assigning them negative meaning. We can be sad when we're sad—and learn from that feeling. We can be angry when we're angry—and try to understand the action to take from that feeling. We can let our feelings come and go and then get back to a natural, positive set point. Not because we need to be positive for everyone else, but because if we can rewire our mind to be more affirming, then we can better weather the harder, stickier emotions.

The other reason affirmations work is because of the repetitive nature of them. By writing the same affirmations every single day, you are teaching your mind how to think about you and your life. It's a way of taking back power over your brain. This might be harder for people who have a mental illness, but I am a clinically diagnosed depressive with generalized anxiety disorder and the Magical Thinking Ritual changed my entire brain. It hasn't *eradicated* my mental illness, but it has significantly lessened its impact on my everyday life.

The final reason affirmations are so powerful is that they will show you where you are out of alignment with your desires. If you're trying to affirm a certain part of your life but are not acting in alignment with that affirmation, then it will become abundantly clear. So, that means affirmations are not inactive. They lead to inspired actions. And they lead you to the gap in what you say you want and what actions you're doing or not doing to support that.

It's a wonderful accountability tool.

It will become clear fairly quickly where you're not showing up for yourself. For example, say one of your affirmations is "I feel energized on a daily basis" but you're not putting in any effort to energize yourself, you'll be able to better identify that discord.

Because that discord, if unidentified, causes a lot of internal disconnect and frustration. You may not even realize it without doing the Magical Thinking Ritual.

How you start with this ritual is you write down all the things you want to feel and have been trying to cultivate in your life.

We'll start with this example: "I want to feel comfortable in my body."

You take your "want" and then turn it into a positive, affirmed state.

The affirmation statements for "I want to feel comfortable in my body" could then be: "I wake up every day feeling good about my body. I love my body and my body loves me. I am very comfortable in my body."

Write it out, as if it's already happening to you. You do this with different buckets, like career, money, body, relationship, and other areas of your life that may benefit from an infusion of hope.

Because I already had a journaling ritual established, I replaced it with a daily affirmation ritual. I started this in 2017 and still, to this day, write my affirmations almost every single morning. I typically write anywhere from ten to twenty affirmation statements per session. I originally started with easy affirmations.

I let go of anxiety and fear.

I allow myself to feel good.

I love money and money loves me.

I love my body and my body loves me.

I'd write these and others over and over every day.

A few weeks in, a funny thing started to happen.

I started to feel . . . different. Better. More optimistic. Less anxious. More confident.

My thoughts started to actually transform.

A few months into writing the affirmations, my mind was an entirely different place. Drastically different. I was amazed. It was like unlocking some secret that nobody had bothered to share. Why didn't *everyone* do this? Why are we all so much more likely to think the most negative things about ourselves? Why do we weigh the negative as more truthful than the positive?

The way we buy into our negative thoughts without interrogating them, I realized that the same could be said about positive thoughts. You can legitimately rewire your brain. You can rewrite your stories. Everything is subjective. Absolutely nothing is objective. Every memory can be interpreted in dozens of ways. Every situation you are faced with can be seen in multiple different lights. We often take our first reaction as the truest one, but most likely it's our most unhealed, conditioned one. It's important to listen to our inner wisdom, but sometimes our inner wisdom is an asshole. It has been conditioned and programmed to think the worst about us.

When I wrote these affirmations, I was rewriting my entire past. I was writing the story of my future. I could actually control how I reacted to the memories, the experiences, and the situations in my life. The negative interpretations I had been inhaling for years were a story I created. I could create a new, positive story. I could expect the best-case scenario to happen in my life. I could reprogram my mind to be *for* me, instead of always against me.

This isn't about bypassing real healing and emotions. It's about recognizing that when something happens to us, we have a choice in how we interpret it. We can make it mean something negative or discouraging about us. Or we can interpret it in a way that allows us to process it, learn from it, and take action from it. It doesn't mean we absolve anyone of consequence or accountability. It means that we don't overlay the experience with even more pain, or make it mean something about our worthiness as a human being.

Writing these affirmations helped me see where I was constantly choosing the most limiting, disheartening, and punishing thoughts and stories. I started writing this one affirmation that changed so much for me: *I allow myself to be happy.* I tried for weeks to get behind the affirmation *I am happy* but I kept having resistance to it. When I started writing *I allow myself to be happy*, I realized that I had blocks about my own happiness. That I was limiting myself. That I wasn't even allowing my own happiness to come through. It's not that I wasn't happy. It was that I wouldn't even notice I was, if I was.

I have taught this method to many people, and every single person who has implemented this ritual consistently has said it has fundamentally changed their life. It's probably one of the most important things I still do on a consistent basis, to this day. When I am feeling off, it's so often because I've stopped writing my affirmations for a week or two.

The thing about our minds is that they are malleable, fragile, and extremely vulnerable to external output. If you are not consciously teaching yourself how to think about your own life, and how it interprets what happens to you, then the world will teach you itself. And usually the world chooses the most heartless way to view external circumstances. If you don't consciously feed yourself positive thoughts, you'll ingest the complaints of everyone else. Our minds are extremely, terrifyingly suggestible.

Writing affirmations has been the only thing that has consistently worked to counteract the negativity my mind is susceptible to. And it's the easiest, quickest habit. I spend no more than ten minutes per day with my journal. I don't write new affirmations every day. I typically write the same affirmations every day for months at a time, mastering whatever growth and evolvement I'm working on in my own healing. The repetition is the most important part. It's the mastery of it. It's doing it so often, our mind has no choice but to change. It's about creating new paradigms and constructing a new lens through which to see the world.

This ritual is a way to be satisfied, without having to do more and become more. But I know for some people that can be triggering. We've all inhaled the societal expectation that we must earn our satisfaction, contentment, and happiness.

If I don't do all the things, then aren't I just living a mediocre life?

How can I be satisfied if I haven't achieved everything I think I "should"? How can I be happy if the world views me as less than, or maybe a disappointment, or maybe even a failure? I can't allow myself to be satisfied! If I'm content, then I'll stop pushing. And then what? What if I stop pushing? What if I stop hustling? What if I stop grinding? What if I stop putting all my happiness onto some future I may never get? Isn't that just mediocrity? Shouldn't we all want to be more than mediocre? If I can just *think* my way into happiness, what's the point of doing all the things, trying to earn my way there?

Ha. You got it. That's the veil, pulled right off the whole game.

Because what if being actually satisfied and content in your life is the total antithesis to being mediocre? What if we changed the definition of mediocrity? Because there are a lot of unhappy people with unfulfilled ideals the world has foisted upon them, feeling like failures who couldn't figure out how to game the system. There are a lot of people who feel inadequate because they aren't famous or the best or living some big, splashy life. There are a lot of people who miss the magic of their everyday lives because they live inside the projected future of a perfect life.

So, be satisfied anyway.

Your satisfaction can be a revolution. Our society tells us our value is in how much we can produce, the legacy we leave behind. It robs us of our humanity, turning us into numbers, instead of humans. It feeds and breeds shame within us. It doesn't want us happy. Or satisfied. Or content. It wants us hustling for our worth, feeling like failures if we can't robotically achieve for twelve hours a day. It has us striving until we're dead.

So, yeah, be satisfied anyway. Write yourself into that kind of life. Realize what a revelation and revolution that really is. Being a happy, healed, joyful person is the exact opposite of a life of mediocrity. It's a broken, ridiculous, sick society that tells us otherwise.

Maybe you'll stay content, just as you are. Maybe you'll never achieve another damn thing in your whole life. So what? You're achieving because you think it will make you happy. But if you can be happy now, just as you are, then you're good. You got it. Go you.

Or maybe it'll do a wild thing like it did to me. I made myself satisfied, regardless of not being anywhere I imagined I'd be. I wasn't the best, the most, the anything. I just wanted to be content. To feel good.

And then, weirdly, at the point where I thought, *Well, I guess this is it, I'll never achieve anything again, oh well, at least I'm happy,* all my desires rushed in to meet me. And all those old dreams I had to let go of in order to find my contentment within, I got to come at them from a whole new angle. I got to start achieving for the joy of it. For the challenge. For the excitement. Because I want to. Because I like to. Because I *can*.

Not to prove anything to you. Not to earn my worth. Not to be a good person within capitalism, within society.

But because it sounded . . . fun. Joyful. Exciting. Magical.

Because when I had nothing left to prove, when I had rewritten myself into a satisfied life, I still had these desires. I still *wanted*. I still had the dream to see just how far my talents could take me, how many people I could impact, how much more fun and joy and love I could contain. I still wanted to see my gifts, abilities, and talents expressed in their fullest, freest sense.

So, be satisfied anyway.

See where it leads you.

Let life be easy on you for a while. Let yourself enjoy your life no matter where you're at. You may come around to your dreams. You'll probably make new dreams. And then those dreams will change, too. It's not a race. It's not a competition. This is not some game that can be won or lost. This is your life.

We are allowed to be happy, *regardless*.

Whatever happens from there, love that.

You're the main character of your life.

You're the lead.

Take it.

Joy for the Sake of Joy

IT'S THE LATE SUMMER OF 2020 and Los Angeles has been locked down since April. I've spent the last four months traversing various spaces in my apartment. My anxiety is loud. It feels like there is no room at all for anything but hopelessness. The world is in pain—the least I can do is give it my pain, as well.

My husband, Houssem, buys a beach umbrella and after four months of being inside, we stake claim on a patch of sand far away from any other humans at Zuma Beach in Malibu.

I remember what it feels like to be alive.

Hours later, as we haul our beach equipment from the sand to the parking lot, I swerve around a person walking on the concrete path that stretches the span of Zuma. I had never noticed this stretch of concrete before. I think to myself: *I should come back here and take a walk alongside the beach.* In the rush of daily life before the pandemic, I never thought to do that. I'd go to the gym, get my workout in, and go on with the day. It was a thing on the to-do list. It never occurred to me to come to Malibu for a walk. Never. It hits me like that—the way a life can feel routine, the way joy can be set aside for days, weeks, months, years.

The way I can feel too busy to be alive.

Like I don't have time for my own life.

Like enjoying my own life is a thing I fit in between the goals and obligations and responsibilities.

Joy doesn't feel important for the first months of the pandemic. In fact, it feels unsafe, selfish, thoughtless. I've spent four months terrified, cautious. Sitting on the beach with an umbrella propped in the sand, a book in my hand—it's the first time in a long time that I feel anything close to joy. It lightens me. It regenerates me. I feel the weight of so much lift off my shoulders. The letting go of that clenching—it feels worthwhile. It feels important.

A few days later, in the middle of the week, I drive twenty minutes to Zuma to walk on that stretch of concrete. I drive through Kanan, a canyon that twists and turns the road, mountains on either side, a view of the water and horizon—one of the most beautiful drives in Los Angeles.

When I arrive at Zuma, to the left of me, as I walk, I watch the roll of waves hit the shore. I feel like it's the first exhale I've had in months. I feel guilty for the delight of it. I am surprised at the sheer joy of something so simple. It's just me, my legs, a couple miles of concrete, and that blue-green water, the white of the waves, the unbelievable blue of the sky, the feel of warmth from the sun, the sweat that starts to pool, the soreness of muscles that have been stagnant, the sand that collects in my shoes somehow.

I walk there on blindingly sunny days, as the last of summer burns out. I walk there on gray days, a hoodie wrapped around me, the wind so strong my eyes burn from the sand that gets in my contacts. I walk there after a fresh rain, abandoning the concrete for the wet sand, the low tide lapping in the near distance. I walk there when there are only a few people on the beach and on the concrete path. I walk there as lockdown restrictions ease, and the beach fills with umbrellas and kids making sandcastles. I walk there on days when the waves are so good, surfers dot the horizon line. I walk there on my saddest, loneliest days, listening to audiobooks so my mind has something else to focus on, getting lost in a story different from my own. I walk there on my highest highs, listening to music so I can soak up the celebration. I walk there when I'm in a bad mood, only to emerge feeling stronger. I walk there when my mind is a maze of conflict and I am terrified I'll never have the answers, only to finish the hour walk feeling calmed.

I walk there so often, and so much, an older, fit couple that I'd never noticed before stops me one day and says, "You are the fastest walker. We always try to keep up with you, but you lap us!" As someone who used to get bullied during gym class for being the slowest person to run the mile, this makes me smile. This makes me feel strong. This makes me feel joy. Stacking up the days. Putting in the work. Giving myself the gift of progress.

It's an uncomplicated kind of joy. Nature. Progress. Steps upon steps. Noticing the way the walk gets easier and easier, and my pace gets faster and faster. Noticing where it used to be difficult feel so much easier week to week. The way I know every curve of the canyon road that I take to get there. The miles I put on my car, driving to the beach. The way I know exactly which traffic light to make a U-turn at, exactly where to park for free on the side of the Pacific Coast Highway where there's an easy opening. The way it goes from being a place I like to go to feeling like it's *my* beach. The way I know that if I'm in a weird mental place, I can go to my beach, take that walk, and feel changed. The way I know that if I take that walk, and still I feel the weirdness or tightness of that emotion, I can look at it, but knowing that most likely the tightness will fade, and I won't even remember what I felt weird about to begin with.

The way it is is joy for the sake of joy.

I am not trying to become a world-class runner. I don't track my walks. Some days, I need something slow and easy. Other days, I want to challenge myself to walk faster. It's for me. I do this thing for me. I don't need to monetize it, or commercialize it, or have it be anything other than an uncomplicated place I can go to materialize joy for myself.

Joy for the sake of joy.

I don't have to earn this walk. Or use it to earn something else. I am not trying to make this beach walk anything more than it is. A way to come home to myself. A joy that is free and easy. A place to go when I am feeling any kind of emotion.

I have written chapters of this book on my phone sitting on the concrete wall where the sand begins. I have written probably half of my Instagram posts at that beach. I have spent a lot of time there, a lot of hours, a lot of pictures taken of the exact same horizon, over and over, in every type of weather.

Over the months, as I kept going to that beach, eschewing my home gym (and eventually the actual gym) in favor of outdoor walks and nature, a seed of something began to take root. More and more, I found that my joy was gaining importance. I made time in my schedule to experience joy. I gave it space to thrive, to bloom. I had never done that before. Not in this kind of conscious way. Not to the extent where it felt like the most important part of my life.

For so long, I believed that joy was something I needed to earn, or, at least, something that I could not create for myself. I thought that, to be alive and to witness the injustices of this world means that there is no place for joy. Joy would mean I'm not paying attention.

But over those months of walking on the beach, I recognized that joy for the sake of joy is a vital imperative. It's how we can thrive in a world that makes it difficult to even survive. It doesn't mean turning off the tap of your empathy, but giving back to yourself, replenishing yourself.

Joy for the sake of joy is the whole point.

It doesn't mean we do not care, or that we are not paying attention. It means that it has to all belong. To live wide awake, we need our joy like we need water, food, sleep. It keeps us going. It gives us purpose. Without joy, why do anything?

Once we stop the proving, the striving, the hustling—all the things we think we need to do in order to earn the right to exist—there is joy. There is joy, uncomplicated. There is joy, unconditionally. There is joy, just for the sake of feeling it. Just because we *can* feel it. Just because it exists. Just because *we* exist.

Don't hold out on joy. Don't dole it out in small quantities. Don't earn it. Don't wait for it. Don't put it on layaway until you've achieved "enough" or have some idealized body. Stop giving it to yourself in microdoses.

Give yourself all the joy. Reckless amounts of it. Cover yourself in joy. Cover yourself in love. You will not lose your way. You will *find* your way there.

When all is lost, return to joy.

When everything is too much, return to joy.

When it looks hopeless, return to joy.

Make joy your priority. Make joy a daily occurrence. Put yourself in the way of joy. Create joy. Build joy. Curate joy. Joy for the sake of joy is a gift we get every single day. Stop giving yourself teaspoons of it at a time, when you can have as much as you want. Trust yourself in the joy. Trust that the joy will lead you to the exact places you didn't know you needed to be. Your joy is safe.

At the heart of a radically content life is uncomplicated, reckless joy. The world will tell you that only the people at the top, the people society deems "good enough," get to have all the joy. But, you don't have to listen to the world. The world does not know you better than you know yourself. Opt out of that thinking. You get to decide who you are. You get to decide what matters to you. You get to decide what value you have, what your worth is, what a "good" life looks and feels like—to you. That is your power. Don't forget it. Don't waste it. Stop believing the world over yourself. You are a world of your own. An entire universe.

Joy for the sake of joy is a reclamation. It's a revolution. It's the basis of a radically content life. Seize it. It's free for you. No matter who we are, what our past is like, where we've come from—we are all capable of creating joy. And that makes joy the most equitable state.

It's available to all of us, any time.

And the lucky ones who experience that kind of reckless, radical joy?

They're simply the ones who have figured it out.

That it's available to them, anytime, anywhere.

They know the importance of joy for the sake of joy.

And now you do, too.

I've spent too much of my life waiting. Waiting to be successful. Waiting to be thin. Waiting for everything to line up. Waiting for the book deal. Waiting to be worthy. Waiting to get to some vague future scenario where everything was perfect and I could finally live my life.

Waiting to live. Waiting to earn my joy. My satisfaction. My contentment.

In many ways, it was a waiting for permission. Societal permission that would swoop in and tell me: "Okay, you've checked off all the boxes, now you can go be happy." This wasn't conscious. It was beyond that. It was an internalized belief about what I had been told the world demanded of me. What my culture wanted from me. What Western society tells me to value. Why enjoy your life if your life isn't impressive to others? You are only as good as you are better than someone else.

Do you notice that? How we create hierarchies? How we evaluate the value of our life based on how it measures up to someone else's? Well, at least my marriage isn't like *their* marriage. At least I'm doing better than *that* neighbor. I may not be perfect, but at least I'm not like *that* woman. Not only do we compare to feel bad about ourselves, but we compare to feel good about ourselves, too. This puts us all in a top-down system. A game of who is doing better than someone else. A race. A structure that pits us against each other, clawing for domination and power—at least we're on top. At least we're better. At least. At least. At least.

But, is that the kind of expansive life we crave?

It wasn't for me. Even though I played the game for a long time. Even though I found myself addicted to the purgatory of waiting for my life to get good.

That's what I waited for: permission.

Permission to love myself and my body. Permission to be happy. Permission to experience joy. Permission to be free. The idea that it's all out there, waiting to be earned.

It's not a conclusion I came to on my own. As I began to unlearn these concepts, it became startlingly clear how much I had picked up from media—in magazines, in TV shows, in movies. Media creates the tapestry of worth and value. And growing up, all I learned was that my happiness was five, ten, twenty pounds from now, could be found in a perfect relationship, and is only available to those who are achieving all their dreams with hustle and hard work. Even innocuous advice like "getting the summer body" gives a subtle indication of who is worthy of summer fun. Summer is only available to those with the "right" body? Summer can only be fun once you've whittled yourself down into that shape? It might seem harmless, but the barrage of it all, the ubiquity of it—that's what creates the harm. It's inescapable.

What are you waiting for? Who is coming to give you permission? It's a radical act to stop waiting, to give yourself the permission you've been waiting for. All the pieces of yourself you've put on layaway—bring them back in. Trust yourself. Love yourself radically. Nobody out there gets to decide who you are. Nobody out there gets to tell you what you're worth. This world may try to make you believe other people hold the power over you, but they don't. When you take it all back within, you realize they never had any power to begin with. You realize that there is a fiery revolution inside of you—just waiting to be sparked.

Light the match.

ABOUT THE AUTHOR

JAMIE VARON'S WRITING has been seen across the internet for over a decade, from her early days of personal blogging all the way to features in publications such as *Teen Vogue*, *HuffPost*, *GOOD*, *Complex*, and many more. Over the years, both her long-form essays and her short-form prose, using her signature style of combining personal story with universal themes, have garnered millions of reads and views. Jamie also shares her thoughts on building a life you really love with her many followers on Facebook, Instagram, and Twitter (@jamievaron). In addition to her writing, she has a long-standing career as a branding expert, course creator, and graphic designer. Her website is jamievaron.com. Jamie lives in Calabasas, California.

ACKNOWLEDGMENTS

I WROTE THIS BOOK in a whirlwind during the summer of 2021, trying to carve out hours of focus at a time when the world had temporarily reopened after lockdown. I tried to give up writing many times in my life, thinking that my ambition felt like a curse. Yet, I now see how it was all leading me here—to when I could write this book with joy and enthusiasm. This book didn't feel "hard" to write. I spent all summer in total chorus with the muses, the universe, the guides and I will forever think of July 2021, in particular, as one of the happiest months of my life. Fully in my purpose, writing with joy, and collecting inspiration like fireflies in a jar. I wrote so much of this book perched on the concrete wall of Zuma Beach, typing into the Notes app on my iPhone.

Inspiration found me everywhere. I felt I was having a love affair with my creativity. Any other time in my life, I'm not sure I would have approached writing a book in this way. For that reason, I have now become a staunch believer in trusting the unique timing of your life.

I want to first thank the community I have on social media (particularly on Instagram), a loud chorus of supporters who always had a kind word, who celebrated all the milestones of this book with such zest, it knocked me over a few times. I feel so lucky that I have managed to amass such a brilliant group of people who think deeply and are in pursuit of growth and evolement. All your DMs and our Coven and community saved me in 2020. I wrote this book with all of you in mind. I wrote this book thinking of how you'd read it, how it would land, and getting excited about you sharing all your epiphanies with me. How I love to hear about epiphanies!

I want to thank Rage Kindelsperger from Quarto who appeared in my life at a time when I was losing a lot of faith. I still buzz, thinking about our first Zoom call. Thank you for seeing me and for offering me a book deal that has already changed the trajectory of my life. Thank you to Keyla Pizarro-Hernández, for editing this book so beautifully and with such care. I believe in the power of editing now because of you. Thank you to Laura Drew for your creative direction—your insights were invaluable and the cover turned out beautifully. Thank you for Kristine Anderson who enthusiastically worked to get this book into as many hands as possible. Thank you to the whole team at Quarto, from the art department to the publicity department. I feel extremely lucky that I got to land with such a great group of people to bring *Radically Content* into the world.

Thank you to my agent, Samantha Fabien, of Root Literary. It was my absolute dream to sign with you—and your tutelage, your wisdom, and your support has meant everything to me. The Aquarian and Gemini bond is magical.

Thank you to Jo O'Neill whose cover designs I gushed over for years. When I told you years ago that I'd love to have you design the cover of my first book, I don't think I imagined it would actually happen. Thank you for designing a cover that makes me so happy every single time I look at it.

Thank you to Marissa Brasko—your friendship is such a gift

to me. Your enthusiasm and support before, during, and after I wrote this book is unparalleled. I feel lucky I get to call you one of my best friends. (And thank you to Maxwell Brasko for being such a light and for reminding me that all the accolades are fun, but being your adult best friend is the real joy. And thank you to John Brasko for being a good sport when I forced myself into becoming an honorary Brasko.)

Thank you to Amanda Crew, for unwavering support, the most healing voice notes, and becoming the fastest close friend in the history of friendship. I can't even tell you how happy I felt when you told me you read my book in a night and couldn't put it down. Our friendship and bond is magical and sacred.

Thank you to the following: Alicia Allen, for being my cheerleader and my favorite Aquarius. Jessica Zollman, for knowing me before, and still loving me now. Sarah Zanotti, for the best three hour FaceTimes on the planet. Ellen Hunt, for being the friend who can always pick up exactly where we left off as if no time has passed at all. Tina Majorino, for our walk and talks and safe spaces. Monique Coleman, for being a soul mate. Lindsey Tramuta, for being my first friend in Paris and my favorite person in France. Audrey Leighton, for the way we mutually admire all the things we've both built. Amanda White, for loving this book and reading it so early. Lucy Hale, for your endorsement, support, and for introducing me to *Many Lives, Many Masters* at a pivotal time in the writing process—that book colored this one in the best way. Kate Baer, for your beautiful writing, and your endorsement that I cherish.

Thank you to my mom, who talked me through every single moment of this journey. When you told me it was time to bet on myself, it changed everything. You are the best mom on the planet. I don't think this process would have been nearly as fun or exciting if I didn't get to share it with you.

Thank you to my family: My dad, for doing spelling bees for me as a kid, and for always supporting my writing with such enthusiasm. My stepdad Steve, for being so excited about this whole process, which made me more excited about it. My older brother Keith Varon, who made it seem possible that you could have a creative career and follow your passion. My younger brother Nick Grutzeck, for showing me what it's like to be disciplined, and for having the biggest heart in the family. Tianna Hope, for always having something encouraging to say, and for being the only person in the family who appreciates my stellar book recommendations. Melanie Buttarazzi, for our deep talks that we managed to have regardless of where we were.

Lastly, thank you to Houssem Zidi, my husband, my partner, my strategist, my photographer, my coach, my sounding board, my best friend. You have never once doubted me. You have never understood where my self-doubt comes from. I love the way you see me as capable, strong, and smart. I don't even want to know where I'd be without your endless support, tough love, and full belief in my capabilities. You are uncomplicated in the way you want to see me do well. It's a gift.

And for all the supporters to come that I will likely leave out, because I had to write this acknowledgement section months before the book hits shelves: I appreciate you so much.